Creating Value as a Senior Leader

"It's not enough to be aligned with the goals of an organization if we're not emotionally aligned with the employees who work there. This concept is not as simple as it sounds, and some of the best executives lack the psychological skills necessary to pave the way to success. Shona Elliott reveals powerful techniques which should be the first things taught in business school but which too often are the last. She reveals the secret sauce of personal connection with team members that every successful leader needs."

**Marianne Williamson**
#1 *New York Times* bestselling author of four
books including *A Return to Love: Reflections on the
Principles of A Course in Miracles*

"As a lifelong student of leadership behavior, I have seen many senior leaders transitioning from love of power to the power of love. Like light, love can be defined both by its presence and its absence. When there is an absence of light we experience darkness. The absence of love translates as the darkness of the ego and its myriad expressions such as fear, anger, aggression, hubris, and hatred. *Creating Value as a Senior Leader* will lead the reader from the organizational dark matter of disengaged and disempowered people to the light of organizational renewal and re-engagement. Shona Elliott navigates the core value of leadership as a relationship rooted in love with great sensitivity and authenticity. The book will be of great value for senior leaders as it provides them with essential tools such as reflection, gratitude, and visioning so that they can lead with impact and connect with their employees through service and empathy.

I have learned from Shona Elliott's work how a deeper connection with employees helps build relationships, trust, and engagement in an organization. I would unhesitatingly recommend this book to senior leaders aspiring for course correction in the second half of their personal and professional lives."

**Professor Debashis Chatterjee**
Director, Indian Institute of Management, Kozhikode, Author of 17 books, including *Timeless Leadership* and *Leading Consciously* and Recipient of Harvard University's Fulbright Fellowship

"Having been a C-suite leader, I know how important it is for executives to lead from a place of connection, a desire to serve and create value. *Creating Value as a Senior Leader* provides leaders with tools, they need to create the conditions where employees feel heard and supported, all key elements of organizational success. A powerful message for all executives to read"

**Heather Monahan**, author of *Confidence Creator*, entrepreneur and podcast host of Creating Confidence

*"Creating Value as a Senior Leader* includes many essential elements of Emotional Intelligence, such as self-awareness, motivation, and empathy; all important traits for senior leaders. Great stories, hard data, and actionable steps help the reader understand the importance of connecting with employees to increase retention, engagement so that organizational goals can be achieved."

**Harvey Deutschendorf**, Emotional Intelligence expert and author of *The Other Kind of Smart*

"Having the opportunity to witness Shona's leadership journey for many years...her book mirrors her own authentic and conscious way of being and what it looks like to lead through service and love."

**Linda Moore**, Advisor and Coach tng

"*Creating Value as a Senior Leader* provides clear messaging and a path forward for executives looking to connect with their employees. A unique balance between research, personal stories, and experience, with a powerful framework leaders can use to transform their organizations."

**Paul Rosenberg**, Award-winning Transformational Leadership Coach and Author of *Rogue Leadership: Harnessing Headwinds to Drive Performance*

"From her personal leadership experiences, to her strong theoretical yet practical approach, this book provides senior leaders, and emerging leaders with important tools and practices to ensure high-performance and organizational success!"

**Sarah Padfield,** Director, Operations and Finance, Faculty of Health Sciences, Western University

"Shona Elliott's Amazon bestselling book, *Create Value as a Senior Leader,* is in true accordance with what really works. Employees are real people, and they (like all of us) desire to be heard, understood, and trusted. *Creating Value as a Senior Leader* helps leaders through reflection, shift their mindset to one where they and their employees can come together for a common purpose to serve each other and their clients. When leaders take this time to listen, to understand, and to have empathy with their employees, wonderful things happen. Ms. Elliott is a brilliant, insightful writer. I highly recommend her book."

**Karen Lorre,** bestselling author of *Chronic Pleasure, Use the Law of Attraction to Transform Fatigue and Pain*, and *Effortless Enchantment, A Memoir of Magic, Magnetism and Miracles.*

# CREATING
# **VALUE**
## AS A SENIOR LEADER

Effective Strategies to
**Increase** Engagement,
**Align with** Your Employees
and **Achieve Your**
**Organization's Goals**

# **SHONA ELLIOTT**

NEW YORK

LONDON • NASHVILLE • MELBOURNE • VANCOUVER

# CREATING **VALUE** AS A SENIOR LEADER

Effective Strategies to Increase Engagement, Align with Your
Employees, and Achieve Your Organization's Goals

Published in New York, New York, by Morgan James Publishing in partnership with Difference
Press. Morgan James is a trademark of Morgan James, LLC. www.MorganJamesPublishing.com

ISBN 9781631952142 paperback
ISBN 9781631952159 eBook
ISBN 9781631952166 audio
Library of Congress Control Number: 2020938579

**Cover Design Concept:** Nakita Duncan

**Cover Design:** Jonathan Lewis  jonathan@jonlincreative.com

**Interior Design:** Chris Treccani  www.3dogcreative.net

**Editor:** Cory Hott

**Book Coaching:** The Author Incubator

**Author Photo:** Ryan Tiehen, Ryan Tiehen Photography

Morgan James is a proud partner of Habitat for Humanity Peninsula
and Greater Williamsburg. Partners in building since 2006.

Get involved today! Visit
MorganJamesPublishing.com/giving-back

I dedicate my first book to my parents, Duncan and Sylvia, as they taught me the importance of hard work, a strong work ethic, and they raised me to always value those who do the work on the front lines. I would not be the person I am today without your love, commitment, and sacrifices to our family.

# Table of Contents

## Chapter 1:

# Another One Bites the Dust

*"One of the tests of leadership is the ability to recognize a problem before it becomes an emergency."*
**—Arnold H. Glasow**

Have you ever woken up on Monday morning, after a brief respite from the daily grind, and immediately thought of all the work awaiting you and your team that day? Your day is filled with projects, deadlines, complaints, budgets to review from your team, poor departmental performance indicators to explain, and off-target financial indicators to resolve. Worse yet, one of your key managers resigned last month, and now your remaining managers are working short-handed. You pull yourself together, get coffee, and head in early to work, hoping you will have some

1

time before the first of your back-to-back meetings to review the reports your leaders submitted to you over the weekend. You get to your office and within a few minutes, one of your highly valued leaders, who is leading several key projects, comes in to chat. With a shaky voice and envelope in hand, she begins what feels like a recited speech, and it dawns on you what she will say next: "Thank you for the opportunity to work for you, but unfortunately, I have taken a position elsewhere."

Just like that, what was already a difficult day becomes exponentially more difficult. Instead of listening to the rest of her prepared "speech," your mind immediately jumps to what manager you can reassign her projects to, and you make a mental note to call Human Resources to begin the recruitment process. Now, out of eight managers, you are down two, and you wonder if this is becoming a pattern—perhaps a sign of a bigger issue that is brewing. Unfortunately, you don't have time to look for your department's turnover rates, let alone review and interpret the data. Looking back, you recall hearing your leaders mention an increase in complaints and a decrease in productivity, saying they too have had a number of key employees leave their teams in the past six months. Again, you think that if you had more time, you would request your team's turnover rates from Human Resources to see exactly how bad the exodus has been, but for now, you need to find a way to transfer the knowledge and information your departing manager has to another one of your leaders. Ah yes, if only you had taken advantage of the knowledge management and succession planning strategies the Human Resources team had discussed last year, you would be in a better position to handle this resignation. Oh, and now you are late for your 8:00 a.m. weekly senior leadership team meeting. So much for getting to work early to get a jump on the day. Happy Monday.

Every leader has turnover; it is inevitable. However, when normal attrition (due to retirements and relocations) turns into key employees and leaders leaving for better opportunities for the same pay (or, at times, less pay) more and more often, you know something is not right. In real time, it is hard to pinpoint when resignations of key employees are a signal of a larger problem. The first resignation happens, and you chalk it up to your former employee wanting a different experience or opportunity elsewhere. Perhaps you blame it on better benefits or compensation. As more resignations occur, you can't shake the feeling that something else is driving your employees from your team. Unfortunately, you can't pull yourself away from the vicious cycle of hiring, onboarding, fire-fighting, and getting the necessary work accomplished while trying to retain your dwindling talent pool to dive deep into the cultural issues that may impact your employees' loyalty.

When you hear your managers complain about being short-staffed, increasing overtime, and seeing performance indicators miss their targets, while perhaps observing market-share loss and decreased customer satisfaction, you know in your gut there is a bigger issue at play. However, as you are on the replace-hire-onboard hamster wheel, you are unable to pause, take a deep breath, and evaluate exactly why your managers are leaving your team.

As you think of a way to dig yourself out of the hole you are in, you sadly recall the days when you were excited at the prospect of being a senior leader. Where you could be in a position to provide value to the organization and make a real difference for your customers, your employees, and your organization. You begin to wonder exactly what the value is that you provide to your organization. You are so busy managing the day-to-day emergencies that you have no time to invest in any of the senior leadership attributes you know you should be focusing on. As you push those thoughts aside, you get to the business at hand and begin to research how to retain employees and reduce turnover. That's when you see the barrage of generic advice on the Internet. While reading the blogs and articles, you feel that most of the advice recommended has already been implemented such as:

- Ensure you have competitive compensation packages and benefits.
- Provide opportunities for learning and advancement.
- Provide work-life balance.
- Administer proper training and onboarding.
- Hire the right employees.

Frustrated by the lack of real help and knowing you had already addressed most of what is suggested and still have a problem, you purchase this book hoping it will make a difference.

You have been a successful leader in the past and you are aware of the cost of high turnover. You know that for every team member lost, there is a significant cost to replace them. The cost to hire and onboard someone new—and the subsequent loss of productivity while the replacement is hired and trained—adds up quickly. Your business incurs overtime costs as a result of working short-staffed while trying to maintain the same levels of productivity. Intuitively, you also know the drain and negative impact on the remaining staff when they pick up the slack and work harder while carrying the burden of training the new team member. Even with knowing the high cost of turnover, you are unsure of how to reduce your employee churn.

Perhaps you are also aware of the indirect costs of not solving your retention issues. For example, you experience missed departmental and operational goals, the decrease in the quality of service or product your team produces, the loss of subject matter expertise and institutional knowledge, the increase in safety incidents, the decrease in staff and customer satisfaction scores, and the emergence of disrespectful behavior, to name a few. This can contribute to a less-than-ideal organizational culture. A culture with low morale, where staff are increasingly engaged in conflict and/or bullying. All these indirect costs impact your reputation, both as an employer and as an organization providing a product or a service. And what about the cost to you as a senior leader?

You are most likely aware of this vicious cycle. You have also invested a lot of time and energy being a senior leader. However, every minute you spend on the replace-hire-onboard hamster wheel, every minute you spend on managing the knowledge transfer of information and expertise from one manager to the next and one employee to the next, every minute you spend trying to find explanations for the increased overtime, decreased productivity and missed performance targets, you know you are not spending that time providing value as a senior leader, which is why you worked so hard for that promotion in the first place. Do I have your attention yet?

Do you dream of better days when your employees were loyal to you and committed to your organization? Do you wish you felt more connected to your team? When was the last time you felt joy, passion, and purpose in your leadership role? Do you long for a day with enough time to properly strategize, and plan the direction for your team? Do you imagine a day when you will strategize and invest time into understanding how you can create more value as a senior leader? Do you desire to create an environment for your team where you are optimizing the potential of every single employee, such that they are working cohesively as a team, providing the best service or product for your customers and achieving your organization's goals? Perhaps your dream is to find a way to get off the hire-replace-onboard hamster wheel you and/or your managers have been riding so you can connect with your team and provide value to them as a leader. It is now your time to focus on the work you hoped to be doing as a senior leader in your organization. First things first, you will need to understand how to break this vicious cycle and prevent further damage to your team and organization.

Given the fact that you found the time to purchase this book and begin to read it, you now know that you need to somehow dedicate the time to solving your retention issues because the turnover cost, overtime, decrease in productivity, and lost market share is too high to lose more employees. Additionally, the failure to retain employees has a significant cost to you as a leader; the cost of spending your time firefighting, hiring, training, and replacing your employees robs you of the time and energy to focus on the work you signed up to do as a leader—to *lead and provide value.*

By the end of this book, you will reconnect with your purpose of being a senior leader and again feel joy in your role while retaining, and yes, engaging with your employees by connecting with them in a meaningful way. You will better understand what changes need to be made to achieve your performance targets, retain employees, and increase employee engagement and customer satisfaction. In addition, you will understand how you can create value as a senior leader in your organization. The good news is that you have already begun this transformative journey. You recognize that you have a problem and are not providing the value you know you can. More importantly, you have a desire to fix this problem, lead in a way that creates value, and show up as the senior leader you know you can be. You also understand that the generic retention advice is not going to get you across the employee retention finish line or put you in a position where you can create value as a senior leader. You started this transformation by picking up this book and are now already on your way to making a difference—for yourself and for those you lead. You are on an incredible path to create value as a senior leader for those you serve. Yes, *serve*. I'll discuss more about that later!

## Chapter 2:

# My Leadership Journey

My leadership style has always been rooted in the belief that leaders are in service to their employees. Although I'm not formally trained in the philosophy of servant leadership, which is a philosophy that great leadership, relationships, and organizational results come from leaders putting others first, I have always approached my leadership roles with the perspective that we have a responsibility to create the ideal working environment for employees to succeed and do their best work. Unfortunately, in the busy world of management, not much time or priority is dedicated to connecting with employees and determining their needs, let alone understanding the environment and conditions in which they work. With the advancement of technology in society and leadership, we have become even more distracted, distant, and disconnected from our employees. Employees make or break an organization and are ultimately the only ones who can achieve an organization's strategic plan, goals, and objectives. Bridging that disconnect by looking at your organization through your employees' eyes helps you, as a senior leader, know what to pay attention to, building understanding around what your employees need to succeed.

My belief about being in service to those I lead came from watching my parents work so hard to provide a great life for our family. My mom went back to school to become a registered nurse (RN) after my siblings and I were all in elementary school. Her stories of being a critical care nurse, taking care of complicated and sick patients, were always interesting to me. I knew from a young age that I would not ever be a nurse or a physician. I was able to see early on how challenging the work was and how little it was valued by administration. Nurses and physicians work twelve to sixteen hours without breaks in some of the most physically demanding and emotionally challenging jobs, caring for those who cannot care for themselves. My mom would come home and tell me about her shifts, how she would chart during her lunch, be pulled to other nursing units where she had no experience, work overtime, and have new patient admissions added to her already-full workload, without ever being thanked. Instead of gratitude, the supervisor would alter schedules and assignments without much notice or explanation, not ever understanding the impact these changes had on her staff (my mom!). Listening to these stories for years and seeing the impact all this had on my mom, shaped my career decisions and certainly my leadership approach. Throughout my career in hospital administration, I would think of how certain policies and leadership styles would have impacted her happiness and fulfillment as a nurse and as a person.

My dad, on the other hand, was in a frontline leadership role for one of the "big three" automotive plants in Windsor, Ontario. Although my dad did not share as many stories as my mom, the stories I did hear taught me the importance of hard work, being fair and consistent as a leader, and always listening to those leaders closest to the employees. My dad would tell the stories of how he would make recommendations to reduce costs or improve efficiencies to his superiors, and when those suggestions were not acted upon, it usually resulted in additional expenses and lost productivity for his organization. My dad was a committed leader, respected by his team, and he knew a wealth of information about the working conditions and reality of the frontline staff. When my dad's leaders did not make full use of this expertise, they missed out on opportunities to make impactful changes that would have furthered the goals of their organization. Understanding these leadership fundamentals helped form my leadership style and principles early on, for which I am grateful. I would not be the leader I am today without their influence.

My first manager role was for a clinical laboratory in the suburbs of Detroit, Michigan. During my second month on the job, I was informed that my phlebotomy team was going to be short-handed to collect the early morning blood specimens from patients in our nursing homes in Detroit. Given that we were running short and both our supervisor and phlebotomy team-lead had picked up a nursing home each, I volunteered to draw blood at a couple of the nursing homes as well. Fortunately, I had shadowed the supervisor of the phlebotomy team within my first month and had an orientation to the set-up of the nursing homes we serviced. In the world before smartphones, I purchased a map of Detroit, grabbed my nursing home assignment list, and set my alarm for 2:00 a.m. so I could cross the border from Windsor, Ontario into Detroit to begin my shift.

After completing my nursing home run, I returned to the main laboratory, dropped off my specimens, and began my normal day of "management." Rose, the supervisor of the phlebotomy team who had been disappointed that she was not selected for the manager position I now held, came into my office with a mixed look of stunned respect and disbelief. She could not believe I woke up early to help the team and draw blood from the nursing homes in inner city Detroit. Rose was appreciative of the help. More importantly, she knew I was genuine in my desire to help and serve. Looking back on my career, I now recognize that my desire to assist and serve those I led started with my first leadership positions. In each of my frontline supervisor and manager roles, I always rolled up my sleeves and stepped in to help my employees.

My decision to pursue a doctoral program years ago was a pivotal point for me. After considering my formal education, which includes an honors bachelor's degree in biochemistry, a master's in business administration, and an advanced certificate in human resources, I felt I was missing formal education in an area that I was truly passionate about—organizational development. For fun, in addition to my day job as a vice president of a 1300 employee organization, I decided to enroll in a part-time doctoral program for organizational development. These studies focused on organizational change, effectiveness, and performance. Through its behavioral science approach, my studies assessed what influences and motivates both leaders and employees.

As part of my doctoral application, I had to submit what my "burning question" was in pursuing a Ph.D. This assignment was easy for me. My burning question was centered around the disconnect of senior leaders from the reality of the front lines.

I had observed this disconnect (and at times as a senior leader been disconnected) throughout my career. The times when I felt the happiest in my role as leader, the times when I felt the most passion for my role, and perhaps the times when I felt I had the greatest impact, were the times when I was the most connected to the employees of the organization I worked for. The better I understood the working conditions of our employees and their reality, the better I could help serve them and make the necessary changes for the employees to show up and do their best work.

I enjoyed the four years of study on organizational change, change management, leadership, and systems, as it academically validated much of what I had learned in my years as a leader. Applied learning and building the bridge between academia and the reality of leadership was helpful for me. I incorporated that learning into my leadership practices going forward. I had completed most of the coursework for the doctoral program when I decided to put my thesis work on hold and accept the role of inaugural CEO for a new organization.

Even though I had put my dissertation on hold, I never lost my passion for being connected to employees on the front line, understanding and improving their work conditions, helping employees and leaders do their best work, and breaking the cycle of storytelling and mythology by management that occurs in organizations. Now, after having stepped backed from the world of senior leadership to care for my daughter at home, I thought I would continue to explore this passion and write about it. In my experience, I believe too many leaders are disconnected from the people they lead, feeling purposeless in their work as leaders. Consequently, they show up every day already busy—attending meetings, submitting budgets, writing reports—but not realizing their full potential as a leader.

## My Connection with Employees

In my fifteen years of senior leadership experience in a variety of roles, industries, for-profit and not-for-profit organizations, and for companies in both Canada and the United States, I've learned that the only successful way to ensure you build a committed organization that achieves its strategies is through a meaningful connection with your employees. Sounds simple enough, right? Yes, the concept is a simple one, but in our fast-paced world of leadership, the consistent execution of this strategy is not. Unfortunately, something that should be intuitive to leaders is, at times, what we resist and avoid. It is easier to hide ourselves away in the office, boardroom, or in meetings than it is to be amongst those we lead. It is challenging to connect with our employees and face the reality of where we may not be meeting their needs. From experience, I know this all too well.

Having worked in a variety of different senior leadership roles and working alongside many talented senior leaders, I would constantly ask myself what value I brought to the senior leadership table. Given that I was usually the youngest of the senior leaders, I knew it was not my breadth of experience that provided the value, nor was it a designation such as RN, MD, PharmD, CMA, or CPA, which was usually a prerequisite to a senior leader role in healthcare. With only a BSc (Hons) and an MBA in hand, I was typically the least credentialed senior leader at the table.

What was my value as a senior leader without the lengthy seniority and degrees? After several years of experience, I began to understand my value as a senior leader. It was my ability to see and understand the perspectives of all stakeholders, to listen intently, to be interested (as opposed to being interesting), and most importantly, to view myself as being in service to others. I could not rely on my seniority, expertise, or degrees to provide value. Therefore, I showed up as someone truly wanting to make a difference for those who did have those credentials and were providing a valuable service to our customers. I learned that to provide value, I would have to listen and ask for feedback to understand others' perspectives as to what we could do better, so they could perform their best work.

As I became more tenured in my career, I constantly fought myself from thinking I knew it all because I had the experience. I had to be mindful about assuming I knew what the problem was and assuming I had the answers as well as the solutions. To continue to provide value, I had to stick to my fundamental leadership tenets that had served me well in my formative years as a senior leader: ask and listen to those who know best. Ask the employees and those leaders closest to the employees. Being connected by listening, seeking to understand the others' perspectives, always asking questions, and viewing my role as one in service to others was how I created value as a senior leader. My focus on closing the loop and following up to ensure action items committed to were implemented was an added bonus.

## My Connection with Managers

In addition to being connected to employees, connecting with managers to better understand what their needs were to be successful was another key area of interest for me as a senior leader. Managers play a vital role in employee retention, employee satisfaction, employee engagement, and the performance of employees. Often senior leaders do not understand what it is they are asking of their managers when they assign them yet another key deliverable to accomplish.

When senior leaders understand how managers spend their time and understand if their time is aligned with the priorities of their organization, it puts them in a better position to know how to support them with the tools they need to succeed. By connecting with their managers, senior leaders will better understand what tools, information, education, and development opportunities managers need to do their work well and feel valued and invested in. Building the business case for a comprehensive three-year leadership development program for our frontline managers and demonstrating its return on investment (when resources were scarce), have been the greatest achievements in my career. It was through that investment of time and resources into our frontline leaders that I equipped and mobilized them to lead their employees to achieve our organization's goals.

By design, and at times by fate, I seem to have landed myself working in leadership roles within organizations that needed help culturally. Albeit by design or fate, I thought I knew what I was jumping into, but most of the time, I did not have an appreciation of the magnitude of the organization's cultural challenges. With each new senior leadership role, regardless of how big the cultural challenges were and how dysfunctional the leadership team was, by connecting with employees and frontline managers and doing my best to understand their world through their eyes, we were always able to move the needle on employee engagement and retention and achieve our organizational goals.

## Having Been in Your Shoes . . .

Given my previous experience being one of those "busy" senior leaders, and at times, avoiding that connection to the reality of my employees, I realized that even great leaders who value their employees get lost in all of the busyness of their leadership roles. When I found myself lost as a senior leader, I challenged myself to reconnect with my frontline managers and employees, and each time, I was reminded of my purpose and calling—to be in service to those I lead. As leaders we all need periodic reminders of why we are in leadership roles to begin with. Our professional lives consume the majority of our time and energy on a daily basis. We all desire to use that time, making a positive impact and contribution to the lives of others. This is why most of us became leaders in the first place.

I know my experience and message will help leaders who are frustrated with either the poor performance of their team, high turnover, or unhappy employees who are not able to do their best work. Most importantly, I know *Creating Value as a Senior Leader* can help transform the lives of leaders who do not yet realize the root of these problems. Having been in your shoes before, I know your struggles and I also know what is possible. Connecting with your employees and frontline managers is a concept and philosophy that doesn't cost a penny. It has basically zero risk and only positive benefits for you, your frontline leaders, your employees, and the organization. I want senior leaders to know that there is more to their jobs than the meetings, the financial targets, and the fires to extinguish. There is another purpose. The purpose of serving the employees in their organization, being connected to them, and seeing the world through their eyes. As a result, this creates a culture where employees choose to work in your organization, choose to stay at your organization, and are committed to and engaged with the work they do. By connecting with your employees and frontline managers, they will become engaged in a way that leads them to follow your organization's strategies, achieve strategic goals, and hit performance indicators. Like you, they are passionate about the work they do, they want to make a difference, and they take pride in serving others.

During my fifteen years of senior leadership experience, I achieved successes and learned many, many lessons. In the upcoming pages I will share with you the mindset strategies, leadership tools, tactics, and tips that helped me and the leaders I worked with achieve cultural renewal in organizations where it was desperately needed, all the while achieving goals that we did not think were ever possible. I look forward to being alongside you for this new chapter of your leadership journey, where you can create conditions such that employee retention issues are a problem of the past and employee connection and engagement help you create value as a senior leader while achieving your organization's goals!

## Chapter 3:

# Our Journey Together

*"The only impossible journey is the one you never begin."*
— **Anthony Robbins**

t was midnight and I was on my sixteenth hour of work as part of the management team of a hospital and community laboratory in Michigan. My team and I were working hard processing blood specimens using our newly-implemented laboratory automation system for the first time. Our laboratory was the first in the state to fully automate the front-end processing of clinical specimens with an automated track connected to automated analyzers. After a year of leading the front-end automation implementation, we were finally here for our "go-live" day.

As with any launch, I had anticipated there would be kinks to work out, issues to troubleshoot, and staff questions to resolve, so I planned to be there with my staff, working alongside them until the last specimen had made its way down the automated track to the analyzer. It had been a long few months of planning and testing, with many late nights preparing for this first day of implementation. I was feeling mentally and physically drained. I looked around the lab to see if any of the management team was present. I was pleased to see the clinical manager of the core laboratory in her office. However, I was disappointed when I didn't see my boss, Liz, the director of our laboratory, in her office. Door shut, lights off.

I asked my colleague where Liz was. She informed me that Liz had left as she usually did around 5:00 p.m. Although I was disappointed that Liz had decided not to stay to support her managers on the most significant day in our laboratory's history, I was not too surprised. There had been many instances in the past few years of reporting to her that had left me feeling frustrated. Liz chose to be disconnected from the reality of what was happening with her managers and with her employees at the laboratory. Not being one to ever shy away from saying what was on my mind, I knew I would yet again be sharing those thoughts with Liz the next time I saw her, which turned out to be many days after that go-live day.

Dispirited, I left my colleague's office, threw my lab coat back on, and rejoined my team on the bench, working hard to get the rest of the specimens ready for processing. Around 1:00 a.m., I felt a hand on my shoulder, and to my surprise our esteemed clinical chemist, Dr. Sulis, had stopped on his way out to thank me for working so hard and for supporting my team. Dr. Sulis knew the consequences of not getting the specimens processed and analyzed in time for the residents' and physicians' 6:30 a.m. rounds. He specifically thanked me for ensuring that all the patients' laboratory results would be available by then. I can't tell you how much that thirty-second interaction meant to me. To be thanked for my contribution further motivated me that early morning to help my team get those last specimens processed.

Unfortunately, Liz didn't check in with me for days. She did not thank me or my team for the successful "go-live" and implementation of the first automated laboratory system in the state. This was the tipping point for me to decide it was time to look for other career options. Within a few months, I happily submitted my resignation to Liz, who seemed bewildered as to why I would leave. As my career evolved and I climbed the management ladder in different roles and organizations, I never forgot Liz and her laissez-faire, passive, and disconnected-from-those-she-managed leadership style. It helped me validate the importance of being connected and engaged with those whom I led. In addition, I've never forgotten the power of real-time "thank yous," the kind Dr. Sulis had shown me in the early morning of our "go-live."

This book is not intended to be an academic, theoretical discussion on leadership. There are plenty of books available that cover basic and advanced leadership principles. Having been in your shoes, my intention is to provide you with the understanding and practical tools for how to create and provide value as a senior leader. Some of these tools, insights, and practical approaches will resonate with you and some will not. Take from *Creating Value as a Senior Leader* what works for you and leave the rest behind. As leaders, we all are unique, having our own set of experiences, values, and leadership styles. Building on your foundation of leadership principles, you will know what will be a fit for you in your evolution to be the best senior leader you can be.

It is hard to begin any journey without knowing where you'll be going and what the stops might be along the way. Most people do not begin a journey without understanding why they are taking the trip in the first place. We will spend time ensuring that you are in the right starting place for this journey by encouraging the right perspective and mindset so you are prepared for the work ahead. Moreover, before we begin the journey of creating value as a senior leader by improving employee retention and engagement, we will take the time to understand why you are on this journey in the first place by reflecting on questions such as:

- Why is employee retention important to you?
- What does creating value as a senior leader look like to you?
- What is leaving your employee retention issues unresolved costing you?
- Why are your good employees leaving you, and how can you prevent it?

Deep down, you know good employees leave their managers— those to whom they report—and not necessarily the organization, and you are perhaps feeling you're not providing optimal value as a senior leader, the kind of leadership skills you know you can.

After we have identified why you are on this journey of creating value as a senior leader and improving employee retention and engagement, we begin with the first step: understanding why your employees choose to leave your team, leave your organization, or worse yet, stay on your team, disengaged and underperforming. You have a wealth of information that will paint the picture as to why employees choose to leave or are not as productive as they could be, which will help you better understand the actions that will need to be implemented to create a culture whereby your employees are engaged, excited to show up to do their best work, and are as passionate as you are in achieving your organization's goals.

As is the case for most leaders today, I know you are busy working more hours than you would like because of the never-ending lists of tasks and goals you must attend to. I know you're wondering how you will find the time to read this book, let alone work on solving your employee retention and engagement problems. Hence, the next step will be to dedicate time and energy out of your already busy day to create value as a senior leader by improving employee retention and engagement. Having been in your shoes, I will walk you through the tools and perspectives you need to find the time and energy to dedicate to solving your employee retention and engagement problems.

Once you have dedicated time to solving your employee retention and engagement problems, the next stop in our journey together is what I believe to be the number one thing you can do to engage and retain your employees—to see the world through your employees' eyes by walking in their shoes. Getting out of your office and into the world of your employees by walking in their shoes will provide you with a different perspective. Essentially you will learn to develop insight into the reality of those you lead. Seeing your organization, your departments, and your leadership approach through a different lens—your employees' eyes. This will help you better understand where changes are needed to retain and engage your employees. By walking in the shoes of your employees, you will begin to build relationships with your employees in a different way. They will be relationships built on respect, trust, and appreciation for the work they provide your organization.

As you see and experience the world through your employees' perspectives, you can concurrently design, build, and implement the additional strategies that I will cover in the remaining chapters. This will help you create and maintain great relationships with your employees and create value as a senior leader. Throughout our journey, we will continue to review tools and tactics that will focus on connecting you as a senior leader with your employees, helping you create value to your employees and organization as a senior leader. In Chapter 8, I will walk you through the important tactic of involving your employees to incorporate their priorities within your organization by creating an employee engagement team or council.

As mentioned earlier, concurrent implementation of several strategies can be of great value. As is the case with compounding interest when you invest money, by working a number of these steps concurrently, you will create compounding and impactful change in the environment your employees work, with how they feel about their work, and with how they feel about their workplace and organization.

Understanding what actions to take is difficult for most leaders in the busy world of endless tasks and activities. In Chapter 9 we will spend time understanding where to focus your attention to take purposeful action so that you focus your time, energy, and resources implementing changes that best move the needle forward with respect to increasing employee engagement and employee retention.

If you have been in a leadership role for some time, you no doubt understand that communication is key to any successful organization. In Chapter 10, we will review the difference between information sharing and engaging employees in bi-directional communication. This concept is critical for transforming your leadership practice and your organization's success.

The next stop on our creating-value-as-a-senior-leader expedition together is understanding the usefulness of engaging your employees proactively in your organization before making decisions that impact employees. In Chapter 11, I will walk you through the steps you can take as a senior leader to ensure your employees' views and perspectives are heard before you implement policies and decisions that impact them. In my experience, I have learned the painful lesson of implementing policies, which woefully miss the mark, as I had not consulted with employees in advance of the decision being made. Sharing my lessons learned will help you avoid the same mistakes I have made in the past.

The next leg of this excursion should be a familiar one—employee recognition. Chapter 12 will take you through the value of recognizing your employees in a meaningful way. We will also discuss basic and advanced recognition strategies that may be useful for your organization to implement. Last but not least, the final stop in our journey together is understanding the importance of celebrating not only the successes of your leaders and employees, but the milestones along the way.

Throughout *Creating Value as Senior Leader*, I've woven the tactic that is the easiest way to boost employee engagement and to ensure your employees feel valued—the practice of proactively engaging your employees in policies, practices, and decisions that impact them. Although this sounds intuitive, most leaders march forward, creating and implementing policies and decisions without understanding the impact on their employees and the customers they serve. We will work through the value of proactive engagement and the time saved as a result of involving your employees in advance of finalizing these decisions and policies.

Throughout our journey together, you will learn how to align your leaders and employees with your strategic and departmental goals, along with motivating your employees to positively contribute to your organization's successes. Managers are a vital piece of the puzzle for employee retention, engagement, and productivity. Providing leadership development offerings aligned with the key drivers of employee engagement and focusing on the application of what they learned, you will prepare your managers to lead effectively. Time is dedicated in each chapter to discuss how your managers can help you and your organization achieve your organization's employee retention, strategic, and operational goals.

Perhaps the most valuable and transformational parts of our journey together are the stops along the way to evaluate your mindset. Implementing the steps without the right mindset will result in work that is uninspired, feels hard, and will be just another thing to add to your long to-do list. In each chapter, we will spend time working on ensuring that you are mentally prepared and grateful to be on the path ahead. You have been given a great gift, and it's a privilege to lead those you serve; you have an opportunity to make a real difference for those you lead. You are about to begin the transformational journey to improve the lives of those you serve and your life as well.

# Chapter 4:

# Understand Your "Why" and Your "What"

*"Employees who believe that management is concerned about them as a whole person—not just an employee—are more productive, more satisfied, more fulfilled. Satisfied employees mean satisfied customers, which leads to profitability."*

**— Anne Mulcahy**

t was Thursday afternoon and I was attending an all-leader meeting with our new CEO, Robert. I had worked with our leadership team closely over the past five years on creating the conditions in which they could feel safe to ask the hard questions. The questions that senior leaders needed to hear to help shape our decisions, achieve our goals, and lead our organization according to our values. I had just completed nine months as interim CEO, and even though I was asked by the board to step forward for the CEO position, I decided to pursue my doctorate.

Within the first ninety days of Robert starting at our organization, I began to second-guess my decision to not proceed as a candidate in the CEO selection process. Robert's management approach was an authoritative, command-and-control type, which was in direct opposition to the people-centered leadership style of our leaders. As much as I personally liked Robert, our leadership styles were not aligned, and as a result, I started considering an opportunity to accept a vice president position at another organization.

I had come to love the leaders and the organization I had worked so hard for during the past eight years and was in two minds about accepting this other position. As I sat in the all-leaders meeting that Thursday afternoon, pondering the difficult decision to accept the other vice president position, Robert went to the front of the room and began to speak. Although not on the agenda, Robert began to tell our leaders what he expected from them regarding financial accountability. To everyone's surprise he sternly announced that, on a monthly basis, our managers and directors were going to sit across the table from him so they could see the "whites of his eyes" while having to explain directly to him any financial variances over five percent.

I am all about financial accountability, and I had personally implemented a financial accountability process within my portfolio, which helped drive my departments to achieve their financial targets. What challenged me about the financial directive Robert had just issued to our leaders was the threatening approach he used as a method to ensure financial accountability. Our leaders were accustomed to achieving their financial targets without any threats or directives. As Robert continued with his lecture, I could feel all eyes on me, expecting me to speak up and challenge Robert's autocratic ways, which would have been my usual approach. I saw the disbelief on the faces of our leaders, as they had never been spoken to in that way before. They certainly were not feeling valued as people or as leaders with Robert's threatening tone. This leadership team was a cohesive group, accustomed to working through the most difficult challenges (financial, clinical, and otherwise), and they were used to being treated as competent leaders who could be trusted to accomplish any goal. It was at that moment I knew what my decision would be. Sadly, I felt I needed to leave the organization. I could not work directly for someone who did not share the people-centered, non-authoritative leadership values I and the rest of the leadership team did. I signed the contract that evening for the vice president position at the other organization and submitted my resignation (much to the Robert's surprise) later that week.

## Why Is Retention Important in the First Place?

At this point, you may be wondering why you would be interested in retaining employees who want to leave. Perhaps you have thought, "If my employees do not want to stay on my team, then good riddance; they are not meant to work with me." You may also be of the mindset that you know there are many qualified employees who would be interested in working on your team and would be thankful just to have a job. Easy come, easy go. Maybe you know that losing your employees is costing you but are not exactly sure to what degree. You might also be thinking that you have no control over whether employees resign, and you don't have any influence over their decisions to leave.

You must stop the hemorrhage of good employees leaving your organization. However, you must consider why it is important to you as a leader, regardless of your initial thoughts as to why employees are resigning. Without embarking on understanding "why" retaining employees is important to you, you will not find the motivation to prioritize the retention of employees in your schedule, nor will you focus on the steps needed to help make a difference in retaining employees. As Friedrich Nietzsche once said, "He who has a why to live can bear almost any how."

## Finding Your Why. It Begins with the Data . . .

Every organization captures key organization-wide performance indicators and most likely tracks employee retention by monitoring turnover, both voluntary turnover, when an employee decides to resign from your organization, and involuntary, when an organization asks the employee to leave. Although organizations tend to only focus on voluntary turnovers, reviewing involuntary turnover rates is useful as well. Involuntary turnover can be a sign of issues with the hiring, training, and management of employees leading to the termination of an employee. If several employees are requesting transfers out of a department, this could signal a cultural issue within that department. Although retirements may be inevitable, some employees become disengaged with an organization and retire earlier than they would have otherwise. Reviewing both voluntary and involuntary rates can help you quantify the magnitude of the problem you are facing.

To better understand the impact of employee turnover, some organizations capture the actual cost of each employee separation by factoring in the time and cost involved with the turnover, such as the time spent to fill the vacancy, the hours and weeks in lost productivity, overtime or added shifts, number of lost hours in productivity, and administrative and hiring costs (advertising, resume screening, interviewing, onboarding, etc.). Depending on the study, the average cost to replace an employee could range from sixteen percent of the annual salary for low paying jobs to twenty percent for midrange positions and over two hundred percent of the annual salary for highly-educated or executive positions. Other studies conclude that it costs an organization six to nine months' salary to replace a salaried employee. Reviewing your turnover rates and factoring in the cost to replace an employee based on the information above gives you the financial reasons employee retention is important to you.

## Linking Turnover to Organizational Performance

In addition to the financial and human resource impact each resignation has to your team, recognizing the impact each resignation has on your departmental and organizational performance will also help you understand the full cost of not solving your employee retention problem. When an employee resigns, there is a loss of knowledge and skills, which can be difficult to replace after the employee has left your department. The loss of productivity that occurs when that knowledge and skillset leaves your team can be significant. Furthermore, there is additional cost of existing team members trying to do the departing employees work without that knowledge base. Your management team's time and attention turns from achieving departmental and organizational goals to managing, replacing, onboarding, and training, and organizational performance is often impacted. A meta-analysis of more than 300,000 organizations and units found that "the relationship between total turnover rates and organizational performance is significant and negative." At the end of the day, understand that with each employee who makes the choice to leave your team, you are losing an appreciating asset. The longer an employee chooses to be a part of your team, the more productive they get by learning the systems, the organization, and the products or services provided, and they build the relationships needed to work as a high-performance team member.

## Linking Turnover to Customer Satisfaction

Depending on the nature of your organization, high turnover can have an impact on customer satisfaction. This can be due to the lower productivity of your existing employees with potentially lower quality of either the product or service you are providing related to the inexperience of employees who are thrown into the workplace to replace the vacancies. Studies have shown the correlation between high turnover and decreased productivity with an associated detrimental impact on customer satisfaction. Cornell ILR School Assistant Professor John Hausknecht not only examined whether service quality is impaired by employee turnover, which it is, but he and his colleagues examined the conditions in which it is most damaging. In his study, published in *Applied Psychology*, he wrote, "Large units and those with a high percentage of newcomers had the most trouble dealing with turnover-induced disruption. The more new workers in a workplace, the more problematic the worker turnover, and the more unhappy customers were." Reviewing your market share data, customer satisfaction scores, and key quality metrics and correlating this data with your turnover rates may help you better understand this impact to you, your team, and your organization.

Once you gather this data, carve out time in your calendar to focus on these metrics and reflect on why retaining your employees is important to you and to understand the cost in not solving this problem. Finding a quiet spot free of interruptions, texts, emails, and phone calls to focus on these important questions is the first step in resolving your retention problem.

I know you are looking at your calendar and wondering how you are going to find the time to sit, reflect, and review the data when you have so many other things that require your attention. From experience, I am here to tell you that if you do not dedicate the time to first understanding why solving your employee retention problem is important to you as a leader, you will never dedicate the time, focus, or energy needed to prioritize the work necessary to create the conditions you need to retain your employees—your valuable talent. These reasons will help you decide what to focus on, what to prioritize, what to say yes to, and more importantly, what to say no to when the many competing demands for your attention try to distract you from solving this issue.

Having been in your shoes, I have been tempted to let other priorities dictate where I spent my time and energy. At times, I would put the focus of employee retention and satisfaction on the backburner. It was when I realized the key to improving my customer satisfaction and performance indicators was directly related to reducing employee turnover and improving employee satisfaction and engagement that I decided to make employee retention, satisfaction, and engagement my main priority.

## Self-Reflection and Positive Mindset as Transformational Leadership Tools

Within the first few months of my first senior healthcare leadership role, the CEO I reported to asked me to join him and two consultants he had been working closely with in India to meet with a Harvard Senior Fulbright professor, author, and thought-leader. I was not too keen on leaving Canada and my family to join relative strangers on a visit to India and attend a leadership retreat at a university in a town I had never heard of. When we arrived in India, I experienced a complete culture shock from the sheer amount of people, oxen, cattle, mopeds, and bikes all trying to navigate the roads where North American traffic laws were not followed. This was in addition to staying alone in a sparse room on a university campus and eating food with only my right hand (you can google why you only use your right hand). During the first day of the retreat, leaders spoke about conscious leadership, visualizing your ideal self, leading people through your heart and theirs, and self-reflection. All of this was completely foreign information to me. During the initial days of the leadership retreat, I was exposed to meditation for the first time and an entirely different leadership vernacular than the hierarchal, autocratic leadership language I had been exposed to back home. If I had had access to the Internet, I would have booked an immediate flight home.

My resistance during the first few days of that retreat was intense. I thought the trip was a complete waste of time. I could not believe I was in India, self-reflecting and meditating, when there was so much more important work waiting for me back in Canada. To my surprise, by the end of the three-day workshop, I felt a shift and openness to the self-reflection and visualization techniques I was introduced to. I was beginning to see that perhaps there was some value to this "quackiness" after all!

When the retreat ended, a small group of us were fortunate enough to join our professor on a thirteen-hour overnight train ride to north India. Although we were in the "first class" car, our six-bunk compartment was without doors or curtains, allowing for no privacy and little sleep. What our close quarters did provide was an incredible opportunity to further discuss and visualize what we wanted to create back in Canada for our leaders. By the end of the trip, as I sat on top a pile of rocks in the Himalayan foothills in north India, separated from the group drinking tea, gazing at the majestic mountains in the distance, reflecting on all I had just learned, I was incredibly grateful for this experience, and my hard and egoic approach to management and leadership had been cracked. I began to understand there was a different approach to leadership and an incredible value in quiet reflection and visualization.

My initial resistance to new approaches stemmed from years of being conditioned in a world of authoritative, autocratic, or paternalistic leadership. Having the openness to step out of that world in which we are accustomed to operating, into the discomfort of the unknown where all is possible with the right mindset, is the beginning of transforming yourself as a person and a leader.

Before you analyze the data to assist you in understanding why employee retention is important to you and what the cost of not solving this problem is, it is just as important to take the time to create the right mindset to approach this work. Creating the conditions to help you embrace an ideal mindset for this exercise will shift you from the busy world of managing your day-to-day responsibilities to the world where you show up as the best version possible of your ideal senior leader self. Self-reflection will help create the conditions to help you shift your mindset to one where anything is possible. If you have not had the opportunity to be exposed to self-reflection, gratitude, or visualization as leadership tools, you may find yourself instinctively resisting using these tools, just as I did when I was first exposed to them years ago.

## Creating a Positive Mindset with Gratitude and Visualization

No amount of training, development, new skills, or techniques alone will produce the changes needed to transform your organization's culture into one where you, your leaders, and your employees are all invested in each other's successes and the success of your organization. What you first need is a change in mindset to achieve this cultural shift. Mindset is one of the greatest predictors of success and without the incorporation of consistent practices of gratitude and visualization, it can also be the greatest predictor of lack of success.

## An Introduction to Gratitude

Incorporating a practice of daily self-reflection and gratitude into your schedule will provide several benefits to you as a leader. It will provide a brief respite from the management hamster wheel as you reflect on what you are thankful for that day. Be thankful for the leadership opportunity you have, for the employees you serve, and for those whose lives you positively impact. Robert Emmons, who has spent the last thirty years understanding the science behind why gratitude is so powerful in changing our lives, highlights in his book *Gratitude Works*, "People are 25 percent happier if they keep gratitude journals, sleep one-half hour more per evening, and exercise 33 percent more each week compared to persons who are not keeping these journals . . . Experiencing gratitude leads to increased feelings of connectedness, improved relationships, and even altruism. We have also found that when people experience gratitude, they feel more loving, more forgiving, and closer to God."

The science supporting incorporating gratitude as a daily practice into your life is clear. There are also additional health benefits, such as improving your sleep, reducing blood pressure, and reducing depressive symptoms. Moreover, practicing gratitude not only makes us more optimistic and happier, it helps us become more effective as leaders. According to research, practicing gratitude as a leader enhances your leadership skills to motivate, mentor, and guide your employees (Stone & Stone, 1983), it reduces impatience and improves decision-making (DeSteno, Li, Dickens & Lerner, 2014), it contributes to reduced turnover (Ng, 2016), and it helps us find purpose and meaning in our work (Dik, Duffy, Allan, O'Donnell, Shim & Steger, 2015).

Visualizing yourself as the ideal leader you want to be will create the path for you to provide that value as a senior leader. How can you become your ideal version of a senior leader if you can't visualize it? Abraham Hicks drives home the point of visualization by saying, "You are more productive by doing fifteen minutes of visualization than from sixteen hours of hard labor. Yet, as busy leaders, it is hard to pull ourselves from the frenetic pace of things to do and meetings to attend to find the space to quiet our minds, reflect, and visualize."

Visualizing how you want to show up as an ideal leader and providing value to your employees and organization will help you begin to create the ideal leadership team and leadership philosophy you will use to help you move forward. Creating your vision of an ideal leadership team and philosophy will not only help resolve your retention issue, it will also help you become the leader you always wanted to be. It is *your* vision and understanding *your* why that will help you transform your leadership style, your interaction with your employees, and as a result, your organization's success.

## Starting with Gratitude

Once you have carved out the time on your schedule for this work, find a quiet space in which you will not be interrupted and begin with taking a few deep breaths to help you shift to a state of calm and focus. Next, identify three to five things you are grateful for in your life. Depending on your state of mind in that moment, you may need to ask yourself the question a few times before the answers emerge. If that is the case, do not judge yourself or the answers that come to mind. Next, ask yourself what you are grateful for as a leader within your organization and then ask what three to five things you are grateful for regarding your employees.

My responses would vary from day to day and generally consisted of the following: "I am grateful to get the opportunity to make a difference for those I lead. I am grateful for the opportunity to make positive changes that impact both the employees I serve and the customers of our organization. I am thankful I am in a position to understand what needs to be changed within my department and thankful I am in the position to make these changes. I am grateful for the employees who show up to work every day, day in and day out, grinding it out regardless of how they feel and the conditions they work in. I am grateful for the employees who show up and make a difference to the customers they serve."

When practicing gratitude, I found journaling helpful. There are many different approaches to journaling, and I personally found the stream of consciousness—not letting the pen leave the paper or your fingers leave the keyboard—unstructured, unedited approach quite helpful for me. When I practice gratitude in this way, I avoid judging what I am writing, and I write for a set period of time. It is surprising what insights and "aha" moments are revealed on paper after only five or ten minutes of writing about gratitude in a stream of consciousness state. Others prefer dictating into an app or using a structured approach answering the same two or three questions every day. Experiment with a few tools to see what works best for you. When practicing gratitude, there is no right or wrong approach to enhancing your quality of life, both personally and professionally. Taking this time to identify what you are thankful for helps to move you into a positive state to help you with the visualization activity ahead.

## Visualizing Your Ideal Senior Leader Within

Now that we have shifted into a positive state of mind through the gratitude practice, our next step is visualizing what your ideal leadership style would be when you are at your best and not weighed down by your twelve- to fourteen-hour days of endless meetings.

For me, visualizing who I was as a senior leader when I was at my best—when I had adequate sleep, proper nutrition, exercise, connection to God, and alignment with my purpose as a senior leader—was helpful to me in showing up and being the best senior leader I could be. Until I carved out space to reflect on who I was as a leader, why I was leading, and visualized what my ideal version of my senior leader self was, I continued on the management hamster wheel. I was always in reaction mode and managing the never-ending, relentless onslaught of "stuff" I needed to get done. This was opposed to looking at my role through the lens of gratitude and with the clarity of how I wanted to lead when I was at my best. Once you take the time to visualize who you want to be as a senior leader when you are at your best and visualize the environment you want to create for your employees so they can be at their best, you will approach your work, responsibilities, and meetings differently. You will have more clarity about what the important work is, the work that needs to be done to accomplish your vision of being an ideal senior leader, which is creating and providing value to the employees you are in service to.

As you begin to visualize your answer to the question, "*What does being an ideal senior leader look like to me?*" you can journal your response to this question or just sit back and visualize for five to ten minutes. Specificity is key for this exercise. Envision the details with this exercise. Self-judgment is not allowed; just let the words flow, and let the vision of your ideal senior leader within you get the chance to have a voice. More often than not, we are too busy to take the time to reflect on who we are as leaders or the leaders we always wanted to be. As you visualize and get clear on *what* your ideal senior leader self looks like when you are at your best, begin to think about when you worked on the front lines of your organization. Who was the leader you wished you had worked for or hoped you would become? After the first few minutes of writing without judgment, your inner ideal senior leader will begin to show up.

## Understanding Your Why

Before we turn to the indicators you collected, there is one more self-reflection/journaling exercise to complete: journal about why retaining employees is important to you. Again, use the same approach we did with both the gratitude and visualization exercises, and spend five minutes answering the question, "Why is retaining employees important to me?" without judging the words that come out.

Once you complete these three exercises, take the time to read over what you wrote and identify two or three takeaways or "aha" thoughts you may have uncovered. No matter how many times I take the opportunity to complete these self-reflective journaling exercises, I am always amazed as the new thoughts that emerge. I usually have a few "goose bump" moments where I, again, realize why I am here in the role I am in, fulfilling my purpose, and I feel inspired to make a difference for those I serve. I walk away from these moments of self-reflection renewed in my commitment to create and provide value.

## Analyzing the Data

Having practiced these exercises to create a positive mindset, we can begin to look at the data to help you understand what not solving your employee retention problem is costing you.

### Employee Turnover

As mentioned earlier in this chapter, the average cost to replace an employee ranges anywhere from sixteen to two hundred percent, depending on the position. If your organization calculates the cost per employee turnover, then you already know your direct cost and can move ahead to understanding the indirect costs of not retaining your employees. If your organization captures only the turnover rate and not the cost, then you can calculate the annual cost for the turnover of your employees within your division. Calculating the annual cost can be as simple as taking the average number of employees leaving your department annually and multiplying it by the average annual salary of the employees within your department. This will give you a basic average annual cost. For example, if you had ten employees leave your department last year, and their average salary was $70,000, using the research assumption that replacement costs can be as high as fifty to sixty percent, then it would cost you an average of $35,000 (using the fifty percent assumption) for every employee turnover for a total average annual cost of $350,000. This example is a basic one to help you get a general idea of what it is directly costing you in employee turnover annually.

If you want to take the time to get specific about what your employee turnover problem is costing you and your organization, you can factor in the hard costs associated with the employee separation. Hard costs include the payouts for annual leaves of the departing employee, exit interview administration costs, the cost of current employees working additional shifts and overtime, the cost of temporary employees to cover the vacancy, the recruitment costs to replace the vacancy, time to interview and select the replacement, the cost of checking references and background checks, any pre-employment testing costs, the cost for orientation of the replacement employee, and any on-the-job training costs.

In addition to calculating the hard costs of employee turnover, you can calculate the largely overlooked soft costs of employee turnover, which include the loss of productivity of the departing employee (SHRM suggests that existing employee performance is reduced to fifty to seventy-five percent of normal productivity), increased workload for the other employees, lost productivity of the vacancy, lost productivity of the supervisor to manage the vacancy, lost productivity during the new hire's learning curve, lost productivity of co-workers mentoring and supporting the new hire, and lost productivity of the supervisor to coach and oversee the work of the new hire.

In my experience, using the basic average hard cost of turnover as I described earlier was sufficient. At minimum it was costing me conservatively fifty percent of the annual salary per resignation, and this was significant enough to motivate me to do whatever it would take to resolve this issue (without having to take into account the significant hard and soft replacement costs).

## Human Resource Indicators

In addition to the staggering costs of replacing each employee who chooses to leave your organization, there are additional costs to the existing employees who are impacted by the vacancy. As your turnover increases, your existing employees are working additional shifts and overtime during the time it takes to replace that employee, which can lead to employee burn out. Reviewing your other human resource indicators, such as absenteeism rates, safety incidents, disrespectful behavior or harassment complaints, employee morale, and staff satisfaction (which I will dive deeper into in the next chapter) and looking at which indicators are red flags or are trending in the wrong direction against your previous performance or internal or peer benchmarks will help you paint the picture of the total human resources impact your employee turnover problem is having on your team.

## Painting the Picture

Now that you have calculated the direct (and perhaps indirect) cost of when an employee chooses to leave your team, reviewed your organization's data to understand the larger impact of employee turnover on your human resource indicators, organizational performance, and customer satisfaction, and identified why retaining employees is important, you have begun to outline what this unresolved problem costs you and your organization. Documenting your why, along with your calculated cost of turnover and impact to your organizational performance and customer satisfaction, will assist you as you move forward with the work in the next chapters. In the Chapter 5, you will learn how to dedicate the time, energy, and focus necessary to resolve your employee retention problem, creating value as the ideal senior leader you have envisioned yourself to be!

────────── **Key Takeaways from Chapter 4** ──────────

- The importance of dedicating time to work on understanding why employee retention is important to you.
- The negative impact high turnover has on organizational performance.
- The linkages of turnover to productivity, quality of product or service, and customer satisfaction.
- The importance of positive mind-setting practices, such as gratitude and visualization.
- The use of journaling as a tool for gratitude and visualization practices.
- Identifying what you are grateful for in your role as leader, about your employees, and in your life.
- Visualizing what your ideal senior leader self is when you are at your best.
- Answering the question of why retaining employees is important to you as a leader.
- Calculating the cost and impact of your employee retention problem.
- Analyzing the impact of employee turnover on your human resource metrics, key performance indicators, and departmental goals and objectives.
- Based on the examination of the data and the output of the reflection exercises, painting the picture as to why retaining employees is important to you and the cost of not solving this problem for your team.

## Chapter 5:

# Understanding Your Employees' "Why"

*"Start the retention process when the person is still open to staying and not after they've already told you they're leaving."*
**—Anonymous**

t was Monday morning, and my boss, the president of our international for-profit organization, had just informed me that the owner of the company wanted to come in to give a motivational speech to our employees that morning. We had experienced higher than usual turnover in our organization recently, and our revenue projections for that month were well behind the expected target. The owner of our organization was somewhat of an eccentric individual, and I was never sure what he was going to say or suggest when I attended meetings with him. The owner rarely met with our employees, and as a result, attendance was high for this impromptu meeting.

There was excitement and anticipation in the air regarding the message he would deliver. The owner arrived, stood behind the desk in the lobby of our main office, and began his motivational message. He began by telling stories about his weekend and how he had gotten his six-figure car outfitted with some expensive accessories. He told us of how he purchased several cases of first-growth Bordeaux wines from France. He then proceeded to share his experiences in trying a number of these vintage bottles, breaking down his thoughts on the impact the terroir and age had on these beautiful wines.

Most of the employees in the room were making $40,000 per year and did not even know what first-growth wines were. When the owner began speaking about how they needed to do more with less and hit the aggressive revenue targets that were in place, you can imagine how "motivated" they felt. The owner left the room, smiling and believing he had inspired the staff to work harder to make more money. Not once had he thanked his employees for their hard work. I spent weeks trying to clean up the damage of the demotivated staff he left behind while concurrently trying to achieve our revenue targets with a short-handed team. It was one of my first senior leadership lessons of understanding the damage executives can create when they are disconnected from their employees. Specifically the lesson of senior leaders not recognizing what employees need to hear to be engaged and inspired. He obliviously had missed the mark. Of course, so did our employees, who failed to hit the revenue targets that quarter. Needless to say, our turnover rates did not improve.

At this junction, you have identified why employee retention is important to you, calculated what not solving the problem costs your organization, and envisioned *your ideal senior leader self.* It is time to turn your attention to the reasons in which your employees are choosing to leave your organization and why they mentally leave your team and "check out." We will review the various tools and surveys you can use to understand the reasons your employees are choosing to leave, choosing to stay, or choosing to stay disengaged while collecting a paycheck. This will allow you to prioritize your actions and build a strategy to improve retention. More importantly, this will help you engage the employees who have remained on your team.

There is significant cost associated with each employee who chooses to leave your team. There is also significant hidden cost to organizations that have employees who stay employed with an organization but are not engaged. These employees are simply punching the clock. Both retention and engagement issues financially hurt your organization's bottom line.

## Employees Who Chose to Leave

Understanding the reasons why your employees are choosing to leave your team (voluntary exits) provides you with an important learning opportunity to identify the actions needed to prevent future losses from occurring.

## Exit Interviews

If your organization conducts exit interviews—a process in which your departing employees partake in an online survey, meet with Human Resources, or are interviewed by a third party to identify the drivers which led to the employee choosing to leave your organization—you will want to identify any common themes that have emerged from the exit interviews about why employees choose to leave your organization. Exit interviews can provide a wealth of information regarding this matter. Understanding what changes can be made within your department, so that your current employees feel motivated, stay engaged, and want to stay, is a gift to you as a leader. Unfortunately, many organizations do not collect exit interview data. Although some organizations look at the exit data, this information is often not shared with an organization's senior leaders, because it has not been made a priority given the plethora of competing data and metrics that senior leaders review.

If your organization uses a third party to capture employee exit interview data, you will most likely get a report that highlights the main themes or trends as to why employees choose to leave. Unfortunately, many leaders do not take the time to scrutinize this information, and if they do, they become defensive regarding what the feedback says. Typically, in the exit interview process, the interviewee is kept anonymous; however, sometimes, due to a company's small size, leaders/managers figure out which former employee provided the feedback and tend to discount the information due to their bias toward that individual. This is where exit interviews fail to provide their full potential benefit of getting a true sense of how employees felt about their work environment. This prevents you from identifying and implementing corrective strategies to improve retention.

Other ways your organization may embark on exit interviews is through face-to-face interviews, internal surveys, or questionnaires. Regardless of the format, reviewing the data, themes, and highlights from these interviews can be extremely helpful in identifying what may or may not be working, whether it be leadership development opportunities, organization-wide challenges, and opportunities for improvement.

If your organization is currently not conducting employee exit interviews, inquire with Human Resources or the individual to whom you report. Ask about collecting this data going forward so that a thoughtful exit interview process can be implemented. This is yet another tool in your people-centric toolkit that demonstrates employee voices do count and that you are interested in hearing what employees have to say, whether they stay or leave.

## Stay Interviews: A Tool to Build Trust and Proactively Retain Your Employees

Although this chapter is dedicated to understanding your employees' "why" for leaving, understanding why they choose to stay is just as, if not more, important. Stay interviews are a great tool for managers to understand why current employees choose to stay on their teams and within their organizations. These interviews also look at what factors might cause employees to leave your organization. These interviews are not long, usually thirty minutes, and are separate from a performance review. Managers ask questions focused on understanding why employees enjoy their work and why they do not. This provides an assessment of how best you, as a leader, can support them in their roles. Knowing if your employees feel their talents aren't being fully utilized in their current roles, what motivates or demotivates them, what your employees are passionate about, what makes a great day for them at work, and what would tempt them to leave your organization, provides you with information you can use to make improvements. The value of the stay interview is in the conversation between the manager and the employee. It allows for the opportunity for the manager to express their gratitude to the employee. It helps to build trust and deepen the relationship between the manager and their employee. It also addresses any issues before they become the tipping point for the employee to leave. Additionally, these interviews identify for managers what they should continue doing that has had a positive impact on employee satisfaction and retention and pinpoints what areas they need to address.

If you and your organization are already conducting stay interviews, looking at the data to understand what is working well is a validation to keep expending energy in those areas that positively impact your employees' decisions to stay. Understanding the trends and themes as to what demotivates your employees, how you can better support their frustrations in their current roles, and the reasons they would consider leaving your team will provide you with areas in which to focus so you can retain your employees before they leave. A win-win.

## From Staff Satisfaction to Employee Engagement to Employee Retention

Although staff satisfaction surveys and employee engagement surveys are often used interchangeably, they are different tools and measure different aspects of the employee experience within the organization. Employee satisfaction surveys assess how happy or content the employees are with their jobs and the organization. Employee engagement surveys seek to understand how committed employees are to help their organization achieve their goals as well as how motivated they are to show up and provide their best efforts to help their organizations succeed. Engaged employees are satisfied with their jobs; however, satisfied employees are not always engaged with their organization. Although there are countless definitions of employee engagement, they all center around the extent to which employees feel joy and are passionate about their jobs, their level of commitment toward their work, and the discretionary effort employees are willing to put forth to help their organization achieve its goals.

As mentioned earlier, many studies have determined that organizations with high employee engagement had significantly less turnover than organizations with low engagement scores. In addition, research over the past decade has continued to show that employee engagement is the one primary source of competitive advantage for organizations. Development Dimensions International, Inc. (DDI) compiled the highlights of employee engagement research into a monograph, providing evidence that organizations with highly engaged employees had experienced significant revenue growth, profitability, increases in customer satisfaction, retention, and total shareholder's returns in comparison to companies with low employee engagement. DDI further articulates that through their four decades of research, "engagement is the primary enabler of successful execution of any business strategy."

Depending on your organization, you may conduct periodic staff/employee satisfaction surveys or employee engagement surveys. I will walk you through both the tools and the information they can provide you to help understand where you need to focus your efforts in building an engaged employee culture to increase retention and achieve your organization's goals.

## Staff Satisfaction Surveys

Staff satisfaction surveys require surveying your staff to assess whether they feel they are treated fairly by your organization or not. Depending on who has conducted the surveys, whether a third-party or your Human Resources department, your results will be compiled in a variety of ways. Most often there will be trends pointing to the areas where you are achieving a target and where you are not. These results are compared to your organization's peers, and at times, to peers across the industry. If your organization is in the habit of routinely conducting staff surveys, you will see how you are trending over time. Most third-party survey companies will compile the data in such a way that the top three opportunities for improvement are identified for you. If this is not the case for your team, look for the questions where the scores are the lowest and pick the top three lowest-scoring issues and add them to the opportunities for improvement identified from the exit interviews. Are there any similar themes between the exit interviews and the feedback from the staff surveys? Usually there is some overlap between the feedback from employees who voluntarily leave an organization and those who are the most dissatisfied.

## Employee Engagement Surveys

Employee engagement surveys help organizations understand the level of commitment employees have to your organization. Are your employees trying to go the extra mile? Do they love their work? Are they always looking to continuously improve their work conditions and environment? Do they understand your organization's goals and are they trying to help your organization succeed and accomplish them? Employee engagement surveys help you understand the connection between your organization and your employees' personal goals, values, and motivations. These surveys also help you understand to what degree your employees invest their energy and effort toward achieving positive organizational outcomes.

Gallup, a global analytics and leadership advice firm, analyzed the differences in performance between engaged and actively disengaged teams. They found that business units scoring in the top quartile on employee engagement significantly outperformed those in the bottom quartile. Gallup specifically noted that engaged teams had:

- 41% lower absenteeism.
- 58% fewer patient safety incidents.
- 24% less turnover (in high-turnover organizations).
- 59% less turnover (in low-turnover organizations).
- 70% fewer safety incidents.
- 40% fewer defects (quality).
- 17% higher productivity.
- 20% higher sales.
- 21% higher profitability.

In addition to this research, a 2019 State of Employee Engagement survey conducted by HR.com and sponsored by GLINT identified:

- Leaders and immediate supervisors make the difference in engagement and over eighty percent of HR professionals linked engagement to trust in leaders.
- Only twenty-nine percent of all HR professionals say their organizations have leaders who prioritize engagement.
- Highly engaged organizations are three times as likely to have senior leaders who prioritize employee engagement when compared to organizations with lower engagement.
- Highly engaged organizations are more than twice as likely to report being top financial performers in their industry.

When you review the compelling research, it is easy to make the case that employee engagement should be your number one priority. Creating a culture where employees are highly engaged not only reduces absenteeism and turnover, it leads to higher productivity, higher customer satisfaction, and thus higher profitability. Understanding the current engagement levels of your employees will help you design an employee engagement strategy that will not only produce outcomes as identified by Gallup but will also help you create a culture where a significant percentage of your employees care about your organization and are personally concerned with achieving your organizational goals.

If your organization has used a third-party to conduct the survey, you will receive a report with recommendations, benchmark data of your peer group, and your trends over time. In addition to providing information on what drives employee engagement in your organization, some third-party organizations will compile the information into the top three areas of action based on their research and your organization's profile—areas they believe will have the biggest impact on increasing employee engagement in the future. A few third-party organizations provide a benchmark report that includes employee engagement data from other organizations who are striving for the best of the best for their employees. Understanding where you and your organization compare to others can help you craft an action plan focusing on being the best in class for your employees.

## Pulse Surveys

Organizations may routinely conduct staff satisfaction or employee engagement surveys annually or every two years, which is a significant resource expenditure and does not allow organizations to quickly see the impact of their employee initiatives. To that end, some organizations have moved forward with conducting pulse surveys more frequently as an adjunct to their annual or biennial formal employee survey processes. Implementing an employee pulse survey process will help you understand if your actions have moved the needle with regard to how your employees perceive your organization, and it will help your managers with more frequent and real-time feedback about where they can focus their attention in helping to improve their employees' perspectives about their organization.

If your organization is currently collecting data from pulse surveys, looking at the feedback from the last two rounds of surveying will help you correlate the data to the trends you are seeing in the exit interview data.

If your organization does not conduct exit interviews, staff satisfaction, or employee engagement surveys, there are other ways to get this information. You could hold town halls, staff meetings, and/or focus groups and ask employee engagement questions such as:

- What do you enjoy about working here?
- What are the greatest strengths of our organization?
- What does our company value?
- What is the most meaningful part of your job?
- Describe our leadership culture in three words.
- How do you define success in your role?
- What motivates you to give your best work in your role?
- Name one improvement that could be made in your work environment.

There are plenty of online resources available to assist you with organizing an employee engagement focus group to help you identify the areas you need to prioritize to improve employee engagement.

Some of the key elements in conducting an employee satisfaction or engagement survey include ensuring confidentiality and conveying why employee feedback is important. Employees will want to know that it will be worth their time, what you plan to do with the information, how they will know they have been heard, and what action will be taken. If you have conducted previous employee satisfaction or engagement surveys, include the actions that have been implemented from the results of the last survey. This will help demonstrate to the employees that their opinions matter, their voices were heard, and action was taken. This will positively reinforce employees' willingness to take the time to complete the survey again. The golden rule of employee surveys is to avoid asking any questions that will generate answers you are not willing to incorporate. If you are not going to be open to making change based on employee feedback, then don't ask the questions. The purpose of conducting the survey is for you as leaders to take action.

At this time, you may have little information to interpret or you have a wealth of information provided by some or all these vehicles discussed here. If your organization has little data, as a senior leader, it may be easy to fall into the paralysis by analysis trap, which leads to inaction. Once you have taken the time to digest the information your organization has collected from exit interviews, stay interviews, staff satisfaction surveys, employee engagement surveys, and pulse surveys, you need to interpret the information at hand.

## Intention, Attention, and Positive Mindset

Prior to reviewing this information to better understand why your employees leave and/or choose to stay while disengaging, we will check-in again on your mindset. In addition to creating the conditions to help you shift into a positive mindset, I will walk you through how to review the data you have collected with attention and intention, for the purposes of interpreting the information through the lens of your employee retention goal.

In 2013, a research study from Harvard's Brigham and Women's Hospital expanded the research on inattentional blindness, the idea that we fail to perceive things that are there, hiding in plain sight. The researchers asked twenty-four radiologists to identify a lung nodule in CT scans of the lungs. These were images they were accustomed to seeing and potential pathology they were used to evaluating. In the last case in the series, researchers had superimposed a picture of a man wearing a gorilla suit shaking his fist, which was forty-eight times the size of the average lung nodule. Eighty-three percent of the radiologists did not see the gorilla, even though eye tracking revealed they had looked directly at it.

Understand that everyone, even highly trained and qualified subject matter experts, are subject to inattentional blindness. Ultimately, to see the gorilla in the data, you need to set your intention as to what you pay attention to. Failing to do so has impact on the perceptions and assumptions that inform the decisions you make and your understanding of the drivers of your organization's culture. Inattentional blindness is preventing you from seeing the information that is staring you in the face. What you think you see, or what you fail to see, can and will greatly impact how you show up as a senior leader.

Setting intention about what you pay attention to will help to increase your focus as you review the employee data, reducing the risk of inattentional blindness clouding your perception. Being open-minded about what your employees are saying as they leave your organization, coupled with the intention of truly trying to understand why they are choosing to leave will allow you to make the necessary adjustments that will help you see the gorilla hiding in plain sight in the information you review.

In addition to setting intention about what you pay attention to as you review your employee information and data, I ask that you embark on an exercise similar to what you did in the previous chapter. Being in the right state of mind is essential for reviewing this feedback. Finding a quiet place, one free of interruptions, is needed so you can fully focus on what your employees tell you through the information you collect. You can start this exercise with a few deep breaths or a ten-minute meditation session; then, proceed to ask yourself, "What am I thankful for regarding my leadership role in my organization? What am I grateful for? Who am I grateful for?" Let the thoughts flow to you, repeating each question for a minute or so. Next, ask yourself how, as a senior leader, you show up when you are at your best. Repeating this question, letting the answers flow and emerge as they will. Again, journaling is an option here if that helps the free flow of thoughts for you. Find what works best for you to help shift into a positive mindset to review the information, paying attention to your intention, helping you answer the question about why your employees are leaving and why they may be disengaged.

## What Is the Information Telling Me?

Now that you are in a positive mindset to pay attention with the intention of solving your employee retention problem, you can begin to review the exit interview data. When reviewing this information, do your best to avoid taking the information personally. From experience, I appreciate how difficult this task can be. Become a third-party observer to what the data is saying, even if it is about you or does not align with your point of view. The key is to understand that this information is your employees' perspective (right or wrong). It was how they felt about their working conditions at the time they took the survey. View the feedback as information only, utilizing what the information is telling you to aid in your decision-making going forward.

From this information, identify the top three things you can influence or change. Was the feedback surprising? Were there any lessons learned or "aha" moments? What did you notice was working well? You can make notes of positive feedback about leaders on your team and take the time to circle back with them. Letting your leaders know what their employees felt was positive about their leadership style helps reinforce that positive behavior. In addition, sharing with your leadership team as a whole what employees' value in leaders helps them incorporate those leadership attributes more consistently into their approaches. Were there any themes regarding leadership styles, working conditions, or the culture of the department in which the employee worked? Often, management will assume that employees leave for better money somewhere else. In my experience, unless your organization's compensation philosophy is significantly different from other organizations, employees choose to leave because they are not happy from a leadership or cultural perspective.

When reviewing exit interview information, you will most likely observe opportunities for improvement for HR policies, system-wide issues, or organization-wide challenges. Inquiring with HR about what is being done with exit interview data from an organization-wide perspective will be helpful for you to understand as you move forward.

Now that you have reviewed the feedback from the employees who chose to leave your team or organization, we need to also look at what your current employees think and how they feel. We also need to evaluate employees who are dissatisfied and disengaged but choose to stay employed with your team. These individuals will eventually leave (this is a good opportunity to listen to them and take action to prevent them from leaving), or they will stay dissatisfied and disengaged, which is the greatest threat to your team and organization.

These dissatisfied/disengaged employees are like a virus to the rest of your engaged and satisfied team. They do not carry their weight and tend not to perform their best. They are usually pessimistic and are not interested in helping others or the leadership of the organization achieve their goals. These disgruntled employees may be quite vocal at staff meetings, town halls, or around the "water cooler" about what they dislike about anything or everyone. However, they may be quiet about their dissatisfaction and have been long checked out. These employees come to put in their time, do the bare minimum, collect a check, and leave.

These individuals are far more destructive to your team and productivity than the churn of new employees coming in to replace those who left. To hear what these employees think, you can look to your most recent staff satisfaction or employee engagement scores, which ideally would have been conducted within the previous year. Again, begin to embark on the mindset exercise where you take a few deep breaths and center yourself, moving to a position of observation—a position of seeking to understand. Take time to pay attention to what the information is saying using your intention of engaging and retaining your employees.

## Completion Rate

Analyzing the completion rate of employment surveys is a sign in itself of trust, communication, and culture. Experts still debate, but the percent completion rate needed to determine engagement is estimated to be around seventy percent. If your employee completion rates fall below seventy percent, further understanding as to why employees are not completing the survey is needed. Questions managers might ask to help understand lower completion rates include:

- "How well was the survey communicated (perhaps signaling communication issues)?"
- "How easily could employees access the survey via email, kiosk, SMS, paper, phone calls, or other means?"
- "Was there potential survey fatigue, as in when was the last time employees participated in a survey?"
- "What is the organizational trust level (did employees believe feedback was anonymous?)"
- "How did the current organizational culture impact completion rates (did employees think it wasn't worth their time to complete the survey)?
- Asking these questions will help pinpoint areas that may need addressing.

## The Numbers, Trends, and Benchmarks

As mentioned earlier, if a third party has conducted the survey on your behalf, most likely you will receive the data results along with your trends in comparison to previous years and benchmarks against a selected peer group and/or a peer group of best-practice employers. In addition, a number of third-party organizations will help you understand what drives employee engagement for your organization based on your results. They will also identify the top three things your organization should work on that will have the most significant impact on improving employee engagement.

If your surveys are conducted internally, and you do not have any peers to benchmark against or any previous survey data to compare with, understanding whether the results are statistically meaningful is key. Based on the data, you should identify three areas of improvement as a good starting point for moving forward with an action plan. There are many ways to identify these improvement opportunities. Holding an employee focus group to help make sense of the information is an excellent exercise in validating how you are interpreting what your employees are saying to you through the data. This will also signal to your employees that you have heard them and value their feedback.

## The Gift of Employee Comments

Many organizations, when reviewing their survey data, pick the top three areas with the lowest scores and take action. Action is great, but there could be a missed opportunity if you do not look to your employees' comments for context of the survey results. Taking the time to read the comments for the purposes of getting a better understanding of how your employees are feeling and picking up on the nuances of their views helps you to better understand your employees' perspectives in a deeper, more meaningful way.

From experience, I know it is hard to read the negative information, which may not be framed or packaged in the prettiest of ways. Rising above the potentially ugly delivery will help you see that this is a gift to you—something you can use to make positive changes to help retain your employees and have them engaged in their work.

If you are afraid this information will expose your weak spots within your leadership style, recognize that all leaders have blind spots and areas that need improving. Again, understand that this information is a gift to you from your employees. Refrain from judging yourself or becoming defensive and lean into what the information is telling you. Try to find the kernel of truth in what your employees are saying. Finding these truths, as opposed to blindly running away from the information, will help you evolve and become the ideal leader you know you can be.

When reading the comments, your employees' voices can be heard. Having the right mindset when reading the comments is especially important. It is the comments that provide the context, insight, energy, and vibe into what your employees feel. As most third parties roll up the data into aggregates and trends, the context and emotion sometimes get left behind. Reading comments from the employees brings it all to life.

Most organizations' senior teams will only see the rollup of the staff survey, employee engagement, and exit interview scores. Depending on the accountability framework and priorities of an organization, you may have already had meetings as a senior leadership team and identified what areas need improvement. If this is the case, taking the time now to ask yourself the question about what ownership you have taken for the results and improvement opportunities will be helpful. As a previous vice president and chief human resources officer, I have seen other senior leaders assume it's only the HR team's responsibility to fix engagement and not their responsibility. Understand that your ownership and dedication of time and energy to improving engagement will have direct impact on engagement itself. Taking ownership as a senior leader for engagement in your team and making it a priority is one of the most important ways you can create and provide value as a senior leader to your employees and organization.

Additionally, as a senior leader, you need to work with your leaders to understand where to focus your energy to develop an action plan to best drive engagement in your organization. As you are working through this information with your leaders, setting up the right environment, free from judgment or consequences, will be important to ensure your leaders feel safe in proceeding with the discovery of getting to the truth of what improvements are needed within their teams.

## Management Effectiveness and the Impact on Employee Engagement and Retention

There is extensive research written about the impact of the direct manager on the satisfaction and engagement of their employees. According to Gallup, managers account for at least seventy percent of the variance in employee engagement scores across business units, yet organizations get shy, or perhaps too aggressive, when it comes to better understanding their managers' effectiveness. In addition, after studying 300,000 teams around the world, Gallup found the one thing that makes the difference between high performing teams and non-high performing teams is the manager.

Understanding how your employees perceive their manager's leadership style is important to gaining clarity on why your employees are choosing to leave your team or are not engaged. For this purpose, some organizations include management effectiveness questions in their employee satisfaction or employee engagement surveys. Others conduct separate surveys specifically focused on evaluating the employees' perception regarding their manager's values, communication style, leadership qualities, or behaviors and effectiveness. Others ask employees to participate in a 360-degree feedback process, where confidential feedback is collected from the employees, peers, and leaders of that manager for the purpose of creating development plans for their managers.

Unfortunately, most organizations do not align their leadership development offerings for their managers with what is measured in employee engagement surveys. Understanding the gaps between your organization's leadership expectations for managers and how your employees perceive the manager's execution of those leadership skills, core competencies, or attributes will help you develop a specific, individualized leadership development plan for your managers. In addition, by studying the trends in the gaps for your management group as a whole, you can create a leadership strategy to bridge the gaps in your employee engagement survey. Strategically investing your education and leadership development training dollars in the key leadership attributes that drive employee engagement, as measured by your employee engagement survey, will leverage those dollars to help you increase engagement, performance, and productivity.

Although direct manager effectiveness is not the focus of this book, there are plenty of online resources available on best approaches for both individual leadership development and how to build an annual organization-wide leadership development strategy. In my experience, designing and bringing in, at minimum, a year-long leadership development offering for frontline managers (inclusive of a third-party coach) was instrumental in helping improve our employee engagement scores and achieving our organization's strategic plan. When investing your valuable leadership development dollars, look for programs that focus on applying and sustaining behaviors. One-and-done leadership programs rarely produce change in leaders. Once they leave the classroom, they do not have the opportunity to apply what they learned, and as a result, lose that knowledge.

At no time should the direct supervisor/manager effectiveness questions, included in the employee engagement survey, result in anything punitive for your management team. Using the information from the survey to discipline or terminate your managers will set your organization back significantly. Any trust that has been built with your leadership team will be quickly eroded. Approaching direct supervisor/manager effectiveness questions in a way that uses these tools for the purpose of growth and development, and not performance management, is critical to the success of these questions. In my experience, helping leaders understand that it is not only "what" they get done that is important, but it's also "how" they get the "what" done that drives the employee culture needle. Understanding how employees perceive their manager's leadership approach is essential to creating a culture that values and engages your employees.

If your organization includes management/direct supervisor effectiveness in their employee survey questions, what are your employees saying? What are the trends? Where do you need to focus your energy on building either individualized leadership plans for your managers or leadership development education and training for your management team as a whole? What trends do you see in leadership attributes, which you may need to plan for development within the next year . . . or the next three years?

## Time to Check In. How Are You Feeling?

Now that you have reviewed and documented the trends, themes, and comments from employees about why they leave and why they are disengaged, compare these themes with the reasons "why" employee retention is important to you, which you identified in the previous chapter. Reflect on what this means to you as it relates to creating value as a senior leader.

How do you feel about reviewing this information? Do you feel heavy, weighed down, or overwhelmed? Or do you feel optimistic? Do you see the areas in which you need to focus your attention? If you feel heavy, weighed down, and overwhelmed, re-shift your perspective and focus to "why" this is important to you as a leader. Look back to what your ideal vision is as a senior leader, the one creating value. Keep that vision in the forefront of your mind, recognizing that you are doing the important work needed to transform into that ideal leader, all the while engaging your employees and retaining them. Knowing you have the power and ability to transform the lives of those you lead by being in service to your employees and improving their working conditions will shift you to a more positive state of mind.

As you move forward through the next few chapters, you will see a methodology that will help you to create the conditions your employees and leaders need to be fully engaged with their work. By doing so, this will help you achieve your organization's goals and create value as a senior leader for both your employees and organization.

────────── **Key Takeaways from Chapter 5** ──────────

- Understand the value and gift of employee exit interviews.
- Appreciate the value of conducting stay interviews.
- Understand the difference between staff satisfaction and employee engagement.
- Understand the cost of employee disengagement to your organization.
- Create the conditions to shift into a positive mindset when reviewing employee exit interview information and employee engagement survey data.
- Understand inattentional blindness and the impact on your perception.
- Build in the practices of intention and attention as a preventive measure to inattentional blindness prior to reviewing exit interview and employee engagement information.

- Review exit interview and employee engagement data (if available) and identify areas of improvement.
- Recognize the importance and impact of managers on employee engagement and performance.
- Teach managers that it is not only "what" they get done that is important, but it is also "how" they get the "what" done that is equally, if not more, important.
- Recognize that most leadership development programs are often very different than what is measured in employee engagement surveys.
- Design leadership development programs aligned with your key employee engagement drivers with a focus on applying and sustaining behaviors.
- Keeping your attention on your intention to create the conditions where your employees are engaged and doing their best work will help retain your employees, improving customer satisfaction and ultimately your organization's profitability goals.

# Chapter 6:

# Dedicate Time and Energy to Connect

*"There is nothing so useless as doing efficiently that which should be not done at all."*

**—Peter Drucker**

n my first few years as a vice president, my wonderful executive assistant, Kim, would schedule requested and required meetings into my calendar. She did her job so well that most of my days would be scheduled with back-to-back meetings for twelve hours, with no time scheduled for eating, answering phone calls, or responding to the litany of emails. Not having had a dedicated executive assistant (EA) previously and knowing Kim was an experienced EA, I went along for the ride.

Many days, I was frustrated by the back-to-back meetings that were scheduled, leaving no time but at the end of the day (usually around 8:00 to 9:00 p.m.) to begin my real work of the day—responding to emails, reading reports, writing briefing notes, responding to issues, and following up with my directors on their requests. Over time, I realized a number of these requested and scheduled meetings were unnecessary. During a conversation with one of the consultants I had traveled with to India, I complained about my schedule and the lack of time I had to do any of my real work. The purpose of our call was to discuss leadership development strategies, which due to my overfilled schedule, I certainly had no time to think about prior to our discussion. During our conversation, I explained my frustrations with my overloaded schedule, preventing me from dedicating time to strategic initiatives. In response, the consultant simply asked, "Why don't you take control over your schedule and your calendar?" The idea stopped me in my tracks. I said, "I can't do that. Isn't that what an EA is for?" She patiently explained to me that my time and my energy were mine to decide how to spend. She added that Kim could not possibly know what meetings were going to help move my priorities forward. If there was an open time slot, Kim would schedule the next meeting request, regardless of how the meeting aligned with my priorities.

It was such a simple solution to what was a significant problem for me. Shortly after that conversation, I spoke with Kim and let her know that I would be managing my calendar. At first, managing and controlling my calendar was definitely additional work, but as I began to examine the meetings I was attending, noting the frequency of them, and reviewing the meeting requests that came in, I began to find available time that I could block off for the purposes of creating value as a senior leader by thinking, creating, and reflecting on the priorities that were important to me. I took that practice with me for the rest of my career, and it has allowed me to control how I spend my time, dedicating my energy to the priorities I want to focus on.

Now that you have completed some of the most difficult work of understanding "why" employee retention is important to you, the cost of not solving this problem, as well as understanding what your employees have said about "why" they chose to leave your team or, worse yet, stay while being disengaged, we can identify how to set aside time dedicated to addressing these issues. Carving out time to do this work is not easy due to the countless fires that need extinguishing and the numerous demands on your time. Understanding your "why" as well as your employees' "why" will help you with the next step of critical work, finding the time and energy needed to connect with your employees to increase employee engagement and improve employee retention.

If you are like me, you are already working more hours in a week than you thought you ever would. Your schedule is completely booked. Perhaps the thought of scheduling a lunch, let alone a bathroom break, is overwhelming because you are in a constant state of firefighting or your schedule is full of back-to-back meetings. You wonder how you will find the time to resolve your employee retention and engagement issues. During this chapter, I will help you navigate your schedule and competing priorities to identify time and energy, allowing you the space to focus on creating and providing value as a senior leader by connecting with your employees.

Throughout my career, I have struggled with finding enough time to get all that needs to be done accomplished. Finding time in my schedule to dedicate to employee engagement had, at times, been challenging when I viewed that work as an add-on to my already full schedule. It was when I shifted my perspective to the reality that connecting with my employees was *the work* that needed to be done, clarity around how to prioritize my time and energy showed up. As a senior leader, connecting with your employees and increasing employee engagement is *the work* to do. It is how you create and provide value. Yes, there are budgets to set, revenue targets to achieve, goals to create and achieve, hiring of key talent and their subsequent onboarding, complaints that must be investigated, and customers to meet. I could go on and on with the endless list of tasks and activities leaders are asked to accomplish within their day. Unfortunately, dedicated time to engage and connect with our employees to understand their working lives and their perspective is often not on our radar.

When I dedicated my time and energy to connecting and engaging with my employees by meeting with new hires a month or two after their orientation into our organization, by participating in departmental staff meetings, and by shadowing them in their roles (more about that to come), I realized the number of fires I had to put out seemed to decrease. We did not need to hire as many new employees because retention stabilized and improved. Time dedicated to onboarding new employees dropped dramatically, as did the overtime, and time spent having to justify the negative financial variances to my senior team. It was then I began to understand that connecting with my employees and their work conditions was the true work I needed to do as a senior leader. It was the work that I needed to prioritize in my schedule and the work for which I needed to prioritize my energy.

Although the concept sounds simple enough, I understand it's not easy. It's not as simple as recognizing that connecting with your employees is the work you need to do as a senior leader, and like magic, your calendar clears, and fires stop emerging. However, understanding that this is *the work* to be done, coupled with your new understanding of "why" employee retention and employee engagement are important to you and "why" your employees leave or stay disengaged, you can begin to look at your calendar and the tasks that take up your time through a new lens, creating a different perspective.

Dedicating and prioritizing time to connect with employees has been a never-ending, self-reflection exercise for me during my career. At times, I have done a better job of dedicating time and energy to this important work than at others. Despite the evidence—the obvious transformation and success my teams underwent due to this engagement and connection—I still succumbed to the busy work of being a leader and did not prioritize connecting with my employees. It was when I felt lost in my leadership role and disconnected to my purpose as a leader that I knew I needed to reflect on how I was spending my time. Most often, I realized I had either rescheduled or failed to schedule the time to connect with my employees. With that realization, I again began dedicating time in my calendar for this purpose. As a result, I felt more aligned with my purpose as a leader, energized again to do *the work* and create value as a senior leader.

Having the gift of time to reflect on what worked well for me as a senior leader and what lessons I learned has been valuable. As I look back on my career, one of my wishes during those years was to have carved out even more time to connect with my employees. My other wish was to incorporate more space and time for gratitude and visioning, as well as for the positive mind-setting practices, which I covered in Chapter 4. Even though I had made employee engagement and connection a priority in my tenured career, having the opportunity to step back and reflect, I recently realized I could have made this a greater priority. The most important work that I did as a senior leader was dedicating time to build relationships with my employees and leaders, seeing their working conditions through their eyes. This allowed me to make the needed changes to improve their environments, changes that helped them be their best. It was how I created and provided value as a senior leader, and it was the work I could have—should have—done even more.

## Yeah, I Get That It Is Important, but How Do I Find the Time?

In the words of Tony Blair, "The art of leadership is saying no, not saying yes. It easy to say yes."

Now, let's turn our attention to the practical task of finding the time (and energy) to connect with your employees. There are more time management tools, blogs, books, apps, and types of software to help you organize your day than I can count. Although these tools might help you organize and manage your time, they may not necessarily help you achieve your goals.

As a leader, you already appreciate that your time is a scarce and finite resource. Dedicating time to better understanding how you spend your time is rarely a priority. Reviewing your calendar and knowing how you spend your time is one of the most valuable strategies you can implement. As you now know what you want to accomplish as a senior leader, you will be able to view your current activities through the lens of your priorities. This will help you to leverage your time and identify what activities do not provide value to achieving your objectives of creating value as a senior leader by connecting, serving, and engaging with your employees.

## Schedule Your Time According to Your Priorities and Goals

Once you have taken the time to review your calendar through the lens of what you want to accomplish as a senior leader, the next step is to understand what your goals and priorities are and to schedule your time accordingly. When you look at your calendar, what activities are predominantly consuming your time? Are you in meetings most of the day? If so, do you need to be in attendance? Can you send another delegate or representative to attend instead? If you don't have an agenda to know what the meeting is about, ask for one from the meeting organizer so that you can be prepared for the meeting and decide if you need to attend or if you are the right person to attend. Instead of spending time travelling, understanding what business you should conduct face-to-face, will help you leverage your time more appropriately. Continue to evaluate your meetings and activities through the lens, "Will this help me create and provide value as a senior leader? Is this meeting helping me achieve my priority of engaging with my employees and resolving my employee retention problems?" Before you agree to attend a meeting or make a commitment to participate or lead another initiative, you need to understand if these requests align with your priority of retaining your people. I started off this chapter with the story about taking control of my calendar, which I did for this exact purpose. I reviewed my meeting requests through the lens of how it was going to help me achieve my top priorities. Any meeting requests that did not align with my top priorities were politely declined or I sent an appropriate representative.

I know that having an "open door" policy is important for accessibility and transparency for your leaders and employees. Unfortunately, at times, the open door becomes an easy place for other leaders, coworkers, or employees to stop for easy answers, as opposed to solving the problem themselves. Creating limits and boundaries for in-office hours when you are accessible will help you be available as well as minimize interruptions during the times you designate for strategic work.

In my experience of continuously honing my calendar to leverage both my time and energy to achieve my priorities, building in fifteen minutes of downtime in your schedule periodically is essential. It will provide you a break for the purposes of reviewing what is next, shifting gears, and centering yourself for the next meeting or activity ahead. Building in buffers into meetings and appointments will also help you with managing the inevitable delays when meetings do not start or end on time.

## Before You Can Start, You Need to Stop (Or Pause for a Moment)

Now that you understand the value and return on investment that dedicating time, energy, and focus to employee retention and engagement has on your team and your organization, you are excited to begin the work. However, my rule of thumb is that before you can embark on yet another priority, initiative, or activity, some things must stop to free up this capacity. Evaluating your current employee retention goals, any initiatives for which you might be the executive sponsor, and the departmental contributions to your organization's strategic and operational plans is necessary to understand where you can free up capacity. Perhaps previously negotiated and agreed upon timelines for specific deliverables will need to be revisited and renegotiated. As I write this, I know how difficult it was to even consider changing a deliverable timeline. My leadership style was "all things are possible, and there is always a way." Having to renegotiate a deliverable timeline would have felt like a setback. During my career, I had to be careful with this mindset because I had the tendency to burn out my leadership team, and at times, burn myself out. Through experience, I reframed my perspective to identify what was important from a mission, employee, safety, and values perspective to keep my team and myself focused on only the initiatives that would achieve those goals; moreover, I found saying no to those activities that did not align was just as critical. Continuous evaluation, through the lens of employee connection identifies what can be paused, put on hold, or stopped altogether. This will help you free up the capacity to achieve your goal of improved employee engagement and increased employee retention and subsequently achieve your organization's priorities.

## Delegation, Delegation, and More Delegation

Delegation is another one of the tried, tested, and true time management strategies. Learning how to effectively delegate is not only about optimizing your own productivity, it is also about optimizing the productivity of your leaders. According to Brian Tracy, a leadership expert, "The average person today is working at 50 percent of capacity. With effective management and delegation skills, you can tap into that unused 50-percent potential to increase your staff's productivity." Many leaders think they already delegate effectively to their leaders; however, when those leaders are asked about how their direct leader delegates, they often indicate their leaders are not delegating enough. Understanding the balance of delegation and micromanaging is key for you to free up capacity to dedicate time to creating value as a senior leader. This is optimized by enabling your committed leaders and employees to contribute to your organization's success.

During my career, I continuously evaluated my practice of effective delegation because delegating without clear instructions or to the wrong leader can do more harm than good. I also evaluated whether I delegated enough and whether I was delegating too much on overloaded leaders. Yes, appropriate delegation is an essential tool in all leaders' toolkits. It is a tool that needs continual, thoughtful consideration and evaluation. You will need to work with your leaders to assess their current priorities and understand if these priorities are aligned with increasing employee engagement and other key initiatives. This will free up their capacity to take on other responsibilities and will collectively help align your leadership team to contribute to achieving your departmental goals.

## Technology: A Help and Hindrance

Are you ruled by your technology and feel like a slave to your emails, social media, or text notifications? If so, setting specific times dedicated to responding to emails can help. Most emails do not need an instant response. Blocking off time in your calendar and setting your availability as busy will help you more efficiently manage your email. It is important to communicate how you can be reached in case an urgent response is needed. By doing so, you can establish time expectations for when you will respond to non-urgent email requests. Answering emails offline is also an efficient way to avoid being distracted by new emails coming in.

There is no shortage of to-do list and task management apps that can assist you with time management. Explore tools that can help you assess how you are spending your time, organize your to-do lists, and block digital distractions. Furthermore, utilizing the screen time apps on your smartphone will give you a valuable understanding as to how much time you spend distracting yourself with social media or other apps. Utilizing apps, such as Heyfocus and Stayfocusd, can block distracting web sites and browsers. Working in full screen mode with distraction-free software will help you stay focused on the activities you are working on. I personally would put my earbuds in and select the critical thinking or focused binaural (brain entertainment) program on the BrainWave-35 app or use a white noise app to help me focus on critical thinking or writing tasks.

## Building in Time to Connect with Your Employees

Once you review your calendar, blocking out time to connect with employees is your next step. In the chapters ahead, I will identify the work that will fill some of those time blocks, but for now, identifying those blocks of time is key. Start by carving out a six-hour block of time once a month for "employee connection," which I will explain in the next chapter. Also block two hours each week for the purposes of employee retention/engagement strategies. Scheduling time in your calendar, with your availability set to "busy," on a routine basis is critical to protecting the time from other activities. If you have an assistant, give him or her clear instructions not to schedule meetings or activities into that time without your permission (a tool I have used throughout my career). Yes, there will be emergencies or other urgent issues that will require you to clear that time and reschedule it for a later date; however, that is your decision to make, based on your evaluation of what is most important at that time. Assistants or others who have access to your calendar do not have the insight to make that decision for you.

I would also recommend building in a daily block of time in the morning, free of distraction, to study your calendar and ruthlessly review how each meeting and activity is aligning with your priority of creating value as a senior leader. In addition, take the time to ask yourself, "What is the one thing I can do today to help me connect with my employees?" This helps you to build daily wins toward your overall goal. By continuously focusing on what is most important to you, your ideal version of your senior leader self, and engaging and retaining your employees, you will create traction and momentum in transforming the culture of your organization.

## Perhaps I Found Some Time. Now How Do I Find the Energy?

Managing not only your time but also your energy is important for you as a leader and as a person. Too often, leaders work long hours, sacrificing sleep, leaving them in a state of never-ending exhaustion. Unfortunately, this "burn the candle at both ends" approach to leadership leaves many leaders physically tired, mentally exhausted, and feeling ineffective and unproductive, which becomes a vicious cycle. As leaders, our energy is constantly depleted. We tend not to give much thought toward how to replenish that energy to help us achieve our priorities. Although not the primary focus of this book, I felt that not touching on this important and often overlooked subject of energy optimization would be a disservice to you.

Professional athletes and world class performers go to great lengths to optimize their energy. They develop strategies, often with the assistance of many experts, to ensure their energy levels deliver high productivity and performance. As a senior leader, you also need high levels of energy every day if you want to create value to those you lead, yet energy optimization is rarely a priority as is the case for professional athletes. Back in Chapter Four, I walked you through the exercise of visualizing your ideal senior leader self—when you are at your best. I specifically included the visualization of being at your best in this exercise because many leaders neglect the essential elements of sleep, fitness, nutrition, mindfulness, and meditation, all needed to help you work at your peak, delivering the high levels of performance you desire to achieve.

With more energy, you have a greater capacity to get things done and you increase your performance as a senior leader. As you optimize your energy, your cognitive and decision-making abilities increase as well. There are many actions leaders can take to increase their energy levels. Focusing on the basics of sleep, nutrition, exercise, mindfulness, and meditation is a good starting place. For those leaders wanting to up the ante and fully optimize their mood, energy, and sleep, "biohacking" might be of interest to you. Biohacking is a deep dive into your personal health and environment to perfect your routine of eating, sleeping, working, meditating and exercising for optimal performance. Biohacking has been around for a while and is becoming more mainstream with people looking to hack their biology to live their most productive and happy lives.

Over the years, I have researched and experimented with a number of "biohacks" in an effort to optimize my energy, performance, and mental clarity. Some of the things I have tried include, intermittent fasting, fueling my brain with healthy fats and polyphenols, functional mobility practices, vibration plates, red light therapy, infrared saunas, blue light blocking glasses, wearing an Oura ring to improve the quality of REM and deep sleep, meditation, mindfulness and gratitude. You should recognize a few on the list. Although classified by some as biohacks, meditation, mindfulness, and gratitude are practices that improve your mindset and have been around long before the term biohacking was created. As previously discussed in Chapter 4, these practices have significant potential to not only impact your health and wellbeing but positively impact your performance as a senior leader.

I am by no means an expert biohacker. I am novice at best. However if you are looking to live your best life and optimize your energy, experimenting with some of these tactics and practices that might fit for your current needs will help you achieve your vision of your ideal senior leader self, creating value for those you lead.

## Mindset Is Key (Again . . .)

While reading this chapter, perhaps you are thinking that this is all well and good, but you have different issues (that I could not possibly understand). Maybe you think this is easier said than done, and you can't possibly find the time (let alone the energy) for solving this costly retention and employee disengagement problem. Whatever reasons you may have (and I can assure you, I have been there with all sorts of reasons) for not believing you can find the time, you need to realize they are limiting beliefs, excuses to avoid the prioritizing of your time and embarking on the work ahead. Limiting beliefs are those thoughts that constrain us in taking action and moving forward. Just by believing and accepting those limiting thoughts, they ultimately become your truth. I am not minimizing or dismissing your important reasons to not find the time, as I have been where you are at many points in my career. In my experience, if something is important enough to us, we will always—*always*—find the time. Therefore, working on your current mindset is critical. When you focus on "why" it can't be done, it won't be done. If you focus on all the reasons you can't schedule the time in your calendar, you will not schedule the time in your calendar. A positive mindset, free of limiting beliefs, is crucial to how you approach this work and the work ahead.

Recognizing your limiting beliefs and approaching this work with a positive mindset is key to moving forward with a renewed energy regarding what is possible and what your ideal vision is of your senior leader self (for help, check back to the initial mindset exercise in Chapter 4). The cost of your time alone, not to mention the energy expenditure, when you lose employees, or they become disengaged is significantly more than it would be if you were to invest the time upfront to solve the problem.

## As Is Mindfulness and Meditation

I always find the story of Gandhi's approach to a busy day a powerful one. At the beginning of a busy day, Gandhi was known to say, "I have so much to accomplish today that I must meditate for two hours instead of one." Another similar quote from Dr. Sukhraj Dhillon reads, "You should sit in meditation for twenty minutes every day—unless you're too busy; then you should sit for an hour." Although incorporating meditation into my day was a practice I had been exposed to early in my tenure as a leader, I had not consistently incorporated meditation into my leadership practice until the last few years in my role as CEO. Even with writing and working through the edits of this book, taking the time to meditate prior to writing always made me more efficient with writing. New ideas and concepts now had the space to emerge without the mindless clutter that was taking up space prior to meditation.

Incorporating a practice of mindfulness, where you stay and live in the present moment, can assist with the prioritizing and focusing of your time. Taking moments to pause and reflect on your priorities, the ones of employee retention, engagement, and connection, can help you receive new requests from a place of stillness. This allows you to avoid the knee-jerk, reactionary response of being pulled into activities that may not be aligned with your priorities.

Incorporating mindfulness is also a helpful tool to assist you with your productivity and energy. Too often, leaders (at times, including myself) are not fully present in meetings. If a meeting is not productive or you feel it is not relevant for you, spend some time focusing on what meeting requests you accept in the future. When we are not fully present, instead thinking about our to-do lists at work or at home, we fail to listen to what is being said. We miss the information being conveyed, which becomes additional work and causes a drain on our energy later. We miss the opportunity to provide value to the conversation and miss being fully informed. Staying present in the moment with others will help you be more efficient with your time, while preserving your energy for the important work ahead.

Leaders need all the help they can get to keep their heads above water with the many competing priorities and demands on their time. Consistent mindfulness practice is an essential tool to avoid the mental and energy-stealing rabbit holes of worst-case scenarios, past hurts and aggressions from your colleagues, and the tendencies to spiral down the never-ending abyss of all that needs to be accomplished. When keeping in the present moment, it is impossible to get lost in the past or become feverish about the future. Instead, you stay productive, focusing on the present conversation or task that you are currently engaged in doing.

Using mindfulness and meditation as a practice to recognizing the negative and limiting beliefs that occur within all of us is a powerful tool to help move through these perceptions. This will open the door to the world where all is possible, and there are no limits to what you can achieve.

As with time management resources, there are plenty of positive mindset resources for you to tap into and explore. If you have not dedicated time to understanding your limiting beliefs, which prevent you from showing up as the best person you can be on a daily basis, and the benefits of staying in the present moment through mindfulness, I listed some resources on my website, www. shonaelliott.org, which may prove useful to you as part of your leadership toolkit.

## Self-Care as a Senior Leader

Lastly and most importantly, taking time for self-care as a senior leader is a must if you are going to have the energy, health, and resiliency needed to achieve that ideal vision of yourself as a senior leader that you created in Chapter 4. Certainly, mindset and mindfulness are elements of self-care, and taking the time to build in other elements of self-care is critical for your ability to be your best as a senior leader and as a person. Making quality sleep, exercise, disconnection from work, nutrition, and stress relief a priority is critical for your longevity as a senior leader and as a person. How can you create and provide value as a senior leader if you are not at your best physically, mentally, and emotionally?

Too many leaders don't evaluate how their time is spent or what consumes their energy. Reviewing your time by asking how it is spent achieving your priorities of retaining and engaging employees will help you identify time that is not aligned with these goals. In addition to blocking off time on your calendar for the purposes of employee connection, which will be the focus of the next chapter, incorporating a ten-minute daily habit in the morning for gratitude, creating a positive mindset, and reviewing your calendar through the lens of how you can create value as a senior leader to those you serve will not only start your day off on the right foot, it will shape how you spend your time and energy the rest of the day. Time and energy that are aligned with your goals of employee connection, engagement, and organizational success!

———————— **Key Takeaways from Chapter 6** ————————

- Recognize that dedicated time with your employees is *the work* to be done.
- Understand that dedicating time to connecting with your employees will free up your time in the long run.
- Declare to yourself, and to those you lead and report to, that connecting with your employees is one of your top priorities. This will help people understand where you will choose to dedicate your energy.
- As connecting with your employees is identified as one of your top priorities, scrutinize your calendar regarding what non-priority items and meetings are consuming your time.
- Understand that you will need to stop doing some things to free up capacity to start focusing your time and energy on employee retention, engagement, and connection.
- Ask for feedback about what your accessibility needs to look like to your peers, leaders, employees, and boss, and communicate to them when and how you will be accessible.
- Review what can be appropriately delegated to other leaders.

- Evaluate your use of technology and introduce tools to help you minimize digital distraction.
- Carve out blocks of time for the purpose of connecting with your employees.
- Invest time in researching tactics, practices, and "bio-hacks" to optimize your energy.
- Build in a ten-minute daily practice for gratitude and create a positive mindset for the purposes of reviewing your schedule and identifying the one thing you can do each day for the goal of employee connection.
- Recognize the impact limiting beliefs have on achieving your goals.
- Incorporate mindfulness and meditation as a leadership practice.
- Understand the importance of building in time for self-care.

## Chapter 7:

# Walking in Your Employees' Shoes

*"As a leader, you should always start with where people are*
*before you try to take them where you want them to go."*
**— Jim Rohn**

You should be feeling as though you have adequately addressed why retaining employees is important to you and your organization, and by now, have a good understanding as to why your employees choose to leave your team and/or organization. You realize the importance of solving this problem sooner rather than later and have blocked out time on your calendar to dedicate to improving employee retention and engagement. In this chapter, we will review how you, as a senior leader, can create value by authentically connecting with your employees, one of the key drivers of employee engagement.

Senior leaders play the pivotal role of defining the culture and direction of their organization, leading them to levels of higher performance to accomplish their mission. Senior leaders typically know everything about the financials, the strategy, their competition, and their industry. However, they may not really know or understand what their employees do in their roles, the nature of their working conditions, and what motivates them. When senior leaders create an environment where employees are passionate about doing their best work, not only are they driving employee engagement, they are delivering their organization's mission. Understanding how you as a senior leader can connect with your employees to better appreciate their working conditions and what motivates them will help build trust, another key for employee engagement.

There are many ways to connect with your employees. Many experts give the advice to connect through social events or holding townhalls. Social events are a great way to build relationships. Townhalls certainly help with conveying pertinent organizational information to your employees. In my experience, there is a more meaningful and purposeful way to engage with your employees. Seeing the world through their eyes while building an authentic relationship with them—walking in the shoes of your employees.

When you walk in the shoes of your employees, by either working alongside them, doing their work, or shadowing them, you are connecting with them personally. You also get to see your organization in a different way than you do by sitting in your office or around a boardroom table. Spending time on the front lines with your employees will provide you an unfiltered view of the reality of your organization through the eyes of both your employees and your customers. As senior leaders, the selective information we hear from our leaders is often sanitized and polished. When you walk in the shoes of your employees, you will see for yourself the working conditions of your employees (the good and the bad) and understand what changes can be made to improve them. As you build a trusting relationship with your employees, they will begin to see you as a regular person, genuinely interested in learning about them and their environment.

## My Experience Walking in the Shoes of Those I Served

I was quite fortunate that my first job after graduating with my honors degree in biochemistry was for a family-run, clinical laboratory. The president of the lab decided to experiment with implementing a new lab assistant classification and wanted to recruit a university science graduate as opposed to the certified phlebotomists they typically hired. I was hired out of a field of over one hundred candidates for this experimental position. I was trained on the job to obtain the phlebotomy skills needed for this role. During my training, I realized this new role came with some obstacles, including extreme dislike coming from the certified technologists and technicians because I was viewed as a threat to them and their profession. There were also personal obstacles, such as having to hurt people with a needle to draw their blood. Since I had no experience drawing blood, I was very thankful that my mom, being a nurse, let me practice on her (the sacrifices only a mother would make!). In addition, I had to learn a new vernacular of clinical laboratory words, which I was not exposed to at the university. I also dealt with my fear of failure while learning to draw blood. When you are learning phlebotomy, your inexperience often causes you to miss the vein and need to re-stick the patient until you are successful.

I was quite fortunate to have been hired in this new position, and I was determined to make the most of it. Knowing I was paying my dues for what I hoped would be a supervisor or managerial position in the future, I spent any spare minute at work trying to learn and shadow those technologists/technicians who looked beyond their disdain to help me. It was these shadowing experiences that helped me form the perspective that to build relationships with those who dislike you, you must take an interest in their roles and their lives. Little did I know how extremely valuable this would be for my future as a leader.

Over a period of six months, I became a somewhat competent phlebotomist and was promoted to the role of home-care phlebotomist. This role required me to draw blood from those who were not able to leave their homes, as well as go to nursing homes and take blood from the patients at those facilities. I was certainly not prepared for this role or ready to experience the living conditions of the patients I visited. Every morning at 6:00 a.m., I began my day with the first stop at a nursing home. I located patients, properly identified them, positioned their arms (at times, needing to creatively secure their arms so they would not strike me), and drew blood, all before they were moved to the dining room for breakfast. Finding patients who did not know their own names in a dining room full of other patients with minimal staff available to help was inefficient and challenging.

Once I completed drawing the nursing home patients' blood, I then had to drive to the first homecare patients, who was typically fasting and waiting for me to draw their blood so they could eat. You can only imagine how impatient some of my clients were if I ran late. Some days, there were two or three fasting patients I had to draw; other days there were five or six. Some days, these patients were a five- or six-minute drive apart from each other, while other days that drive could be ten to twenty minutes. Driving to an address listed on my schedule was much more complicated than it would be today, since GPS and smartphones with Google Maps were not yet invented.

Often, these patients had not had a visit from a friend, relative, or acquaintance in days, weeks, or even months. My five-minute time with them to draw their blood would often become a social care visit. No one had taught me how to respectfully, and with dignity, withdraw from a conversation with a lonely patient so that I could move on to the next fasted patient, who was waiting for me. Some days, I managed to disengage quickly, and other days, I spent the necessary time listening, engaging, and caring, all the while ignoring my pager, calls from the main lab wondering where I was.

There were significant challenges with this setup, and senior management at the laboratory had no idea what they were requiring from their homecare phlebotomists, nor did they recognize the difficult working conditions of this role. There was a reason "homecare" was one of the most dreaded positions in the organization and why there was extreme turnover within the homecare department.

After a few long months with lengthy, overscheduled days, lots of wrong turns, backtracking, and many conversations with lonely patients, I eventually became a bit more proficient in the role. It was one particularly difficult day that got me thinking I needed to show somebody in management what they were expecting of me. I was fortunate that my boss, Mary, was approachable, part of the "family," and trying to better understand the business because her role was more marketing-based than clinical. After this challenging day, I noticed Mary was in her office later than usual, and I asked if I could speak with her. I was happy that she chose to take the time to meet with me, and I unloaded the challenges of my day. I could see that Mary did not quite understand the difficulty in the setup. She wasn't dismissing my concerns, but she was not grasping what I was saying. It was then I decided to be brave and invite her on the road with me for a shift so that she could experience the setup and working conditions herself. I felt that if Mary was truly interested in making a difference (which she had previously indicated she was), then she would jump on the offer to shotgun ride with me for the day. And this is exactly what Mary did.

A week later, I picked Mary up from her office to join me for a partial shift on the homecare route. I had started earlier that morning with my nursing home patients. Back then, I was not bold enough to ask Mary to begin at 5:30 a.m., the time I started my long days. After the first stop at a fasting patient's home in less than ideal conditions, I could already see the disbelief in Mary's eyes about what she experienced and what she was asking her employees to do. As was par for the course, the patient wanted to chat. Ten minutes into our conversation, my pager went off from the lab, letting me know that fasted patients were calling, wanting to eat and wondering when I was going to arrive. Stop after stop, Mary's disbelief and awareness of the working conditions of this position deepened. In-between stops, while Mary navigated the map to our next patient's home, she expressed how unbelievably challenging the job was and wondered how anyone could work in this role for any length of time. She had hit the nail on the head, because the turnover rate for the homecare team, as mentioned earlier, was extremely high. She made statements such as, "I had no idea that the homecare phlebotomy role was this difficult," and, "I did not understand the impact on you and our patients when we (the family management team) increased the volume by bringing on additional nursing homes without increasing staff."

When Mary asked where we would be stopping for lunch and I informed her that lunch was not on the schedule, I knew things would be changing for the better!

I believe Mary shadowing me that day changed both of our lives. Mary had a deeper understanding and appreciation of the working conditions of her employees, and I would use our experience as a fundamental leadership practice throughout my career. Regardless of the leadership role I had (including being a CEO), I made it a priority to shadow or work alongside my employees. I cleaned toilets, washed dishes, prepared food trays on a beltline (a high-pressure role, by the way), shadowed joint replacements and C-sections, worked along ED (Emergency Department) staff on the twelve-hour midnight shift, audited steel manufacturers, and helped service IT (information technology) requests (which I was not very good at). It was these experiences that helped me appreciate the impact of the decisions I made without employee consultation and how those decisions would impact our employees and our clients. I will be forever grateful to Mary for having the open, curious, and accessible leadership style, which created the conditions for me to feel comfortable enough to invite her to shadow me. Mary's interest in learning more about the business and her saying "yes" to walking in my shoes that day were the foundations of my leadership style throughout my career.

When I started consistently building the practice of walking in my employees' shoes into my leadership routine, I did it so that I could have a better understanding of the departments and working conditions of the employees I served. Throughout most of my tenure as a senior leader, I led teams, departments, and divisions in which I had no direct knowledge or working experience, and I certainly had many "imposter syndrome" moments. As a result, I incorporated walking in the shoes of my employees as a part of all my "first hundred-day" plans and, at minimum, every quarter thereafter. By doing so, I could learn more about what my employees did, the clients they served, and subsequently could speak with some credibility around the leadership tables at which I sat. All the while, I built relationships with my employees, made the necessary changes to improve their working conditions, and deepened my understanding of my team's functions. Another benefit of walking in my employees' shoes is that I was able to be a part of my customers' experiences. I could easily see how the working conditions of our employees impacted our customers. As a result, I was able to identify changes we needed to implement to improve both the employee and customer experience.

As mentioned previously, I utilized this foundational leadership philosophy in every leadership role I had. In one role, I went so far to become a certified ISO quality management auditor so I could better lead and serve the hundreds of ISO auditors working worldwide on my team. Conducting audits with my auditors of steel manufacturers, after-market motorcycle parts manufacturers, and automotive tier II and III suppliers helped me significantly in understanding and improving their work conditions. Additionally, by working alongside our auditors, I could directly observe the impact of our expectations of them while they were in the field, making the necessary changes to our decisions to better support them to do their best work.

Having the opportunity to walk in the shoes of my employees in different countries, such as in Japan, gave me a greater appreciation of cross-cultural approaches to work, their traditions, their expectations, and their needs. This deeper understanding helped me retain a significant Japanese accreditation that was in jeopardy, one worth millions in revenue to our organization annually. I am certainly not suggesting you take the practice of walking in your employees' shoes to the extremes that I have; instead, I suggest you start by experiencing what your employees experience on the front lines in any way, shape, or form that feels right for you and your team.

Walking in the shoes of my employees helped me respect and appreciate the contributions of all those I led. It helped me to change the conditions and environment of those I worked alongside for the better. I walked away from each experience humbled and grateful for the privilege to walk in their shoes. Even as I write this, four years out from my last shadowing experience, I get goosebumps thinking of how significant this leadership practice was for me. It continuously deepened my commitment to be in service to those I lead.

## I Know What My Employees Do . . .

You may be asking yourself, "If I already know what my employees do, should I be spending time incorporating a walking-in-your-employees' shoes practice into my already-overloaded schedule?" The answer is yes! Maybe you are a nurse and are now in a chief nursing executive position, or a physician in the role of chief of staff, or a CIO of a technology organization where you once worked as network administrator. Regardless of how well you think you know what your employees do, taking the time to periodically walk in their shoes as a senior leader and viewing their work through their eyes will help bridge the gap between the employee experience and the boardroom. Additionally, you will see how your decisions impact the work experience of your employees.

In particular, a nurse who works his way up the ladder and is promoted to the role of a chief nursing executive may not recognize the inherent microcultures that exist in the different units of the hospital. He may have trained in the emergency department and might not appreciate the differences that working in the OR, ICU, or psychiatry unit present to those employees. The same is true for physicians who work their way up to a hospital administration role; they are specialists in an area and may not appreciate the challenges other specialties have or the microcultures the other specialists work in. Each specialty of medicine is different, and they certainly do not appreciate the roles of the physicians they lead from an administrative perspective. Until they have walked in their employees' shoes and directly experienced the impact of the requirements they implemented, they are disconnected leaders. Removing your preconceived notions of believing you already know what your employees are doing will open you to a new perspective that allows you to see the reality of what your employees do in their roles, providing value to your organization.

## Walking in Your Employees' Shoes: A Practical Guide

There are many ways to embark on implementing the practice of walking in the shoes of those you serve into your schedule. I will list out several key steps that have worked for me. You can proceed as you see best for your leadership style and organization, knowing you will most likely evolve and refine these sessions over time and with experience. Since you already carved out the time in your schedule for the purpose of improving employee retention and connecting with your employees, you are now ready to begin!

- First, identify positions or departments where employee turnover is the highest.
- Prioritize that area to be the first in line for the walking in your employees' shoes experience.
- Create a process to notify the managers and employees of the department that you'll be shadowing.

- Include in your communication, your intention to experience the reality of the working environment of your employees, for the purposes of improvement.
- Dedicate the shadowing time to be uninterrupted, unless there are emergencies.
- Have the right mindset. Define the qualities that make a shadowing experience valuable (being empathetic, listening, observing, being in the present moment/ practicing mindfulness).
- Consider the questions you will ask your employees as you shadow them.
- Identify the means by which you will capture your thoughts and feedback from your employees as you walk in their shoes.
- Create a mechanism to deliver feedback about your experience to your employees.
- Write a thank you note to the employer or employees you worked aside or shadowed directly. At times, I included a gift card with the thank you note.
- Prioritize improvement ideas to investigate, better understand, and implement.
- Create and implement a communication strategy, describing the changes made as a result of listening to your employees and experiencing the reality of their work environment.

## Where to Start?

You have many departments and employee groups to choose from to begin your walking-in-your-employees'-shoes practice and may not know where to start. In my experience, I prioritized the hot spots that needed my attention. I would recommend that as your starting place as well. In Chapter 4, you reviewed your retention rates and would have identified which teams were experiencing higher turnover than others. Select the department in which you have had the greatest exodus of employees for your first experience. It is important to recognize that departments which have high employee turnover tend to have more dysfunction and may not be the friendliest of environments. Therefore, you may prefer to start your employee shadowing experience with a more stable team or a team in which you feel more comfortable with so you can get your feet wet. If you are looking to jump in feet first and time is of the essence to begin to solve your employee retention challenges, then my recommendation is to start with the team or department with the highest turnover rates.

## Notifying Management and Employees

Long before *Undercover Boss* came out in 2010, I had been shadowing and walking in my employees' shoes as a senior leader. Throughout my earlier management positions, not only did I walk in the shoes of the employees I served, I would also work beside them, when needed, to help get the work of the department done. There were many early mornings in the not-so-nice neighborhoods of Detroit where I drew blood in nursing homes when the phlebotomy team was shorthanded. There were also many late nights processing laboratory specimens where I would work side by side with my employees so that physicians' offices had their patients' results before the next day. Unlike *Undercover Boss*, hiding from my employees and going in disguise into their work environment was not ever an option for me. I did not want employees to feel like I was spying on them behind their backs. I wanted them to know that I was there, interested in getting to know them better and wanting to understand their work for the purposes of learning how I could help make improvements to their environment. Transparency of your intentions is the key to a successful experience, which will serve as the foundation to build trust with your employees.

I started each experience by having a conversation with the director/manager of the team I wanted to shadow, explaining to them what I wanted to do and the "why" behind it. Next, I asked that leader for her input about what shift she recommended to provide the best experience. If you have leadership responsibility for employees working shift work and/or weekends, I recommend you consider shadowing those off-shifts. In my experience, senior leaders do not understand the difference in the culture and environment of night and weekend shifts. There is high value from both a leadership and employee perspective to walk in the shoes of your evening and weekend employees.

Understandably, your director/manager might be nervous or anxious about what employees may tell you during the time you shadow or work next to them. Assure your leaders that you will not judge them or look specifically for feedback about their leadership style. Provide your leaders with assurance you will not let the experience turn into a management-bashing session. As you identify a date, the shift, and the employee you will work alongside, work with your leaders to develop the key messages, which will explain to them your intentions and goals of walking in your employees' shoes. Ask your leaders to share these messages as they arrange the logistics of the experience for you.

In advance of your shift, notify the relevant people (your assistant, your leadership team, and possibly the CEO) that you will be unavailable, except for emergencies or time-sensitive issues, during that time. Prepare for a few raised eyebrows when you explain what you will be doing and expect questions such as, "Why would you waste your time doing that when you have so much other work that needs to be done?" Additionally, be prepared for some of your peers, and even your leaders, to be unhappy with your new quest; some may feel threatened. Explain that you want to better understand the environment of those you serve in a deeper way and focus your message on servitude with the hope of improving working conditions.

## Having the Right Mindset

As discussed earlier, define the qualities that make a shadowing experience valuable to you (i.e., being empathetic, authentically listening, being present in the moment, etc.). In addition, setting an intention as to what you will pay attention to during the experience will help you see what is important for the purposes of connecting with your employees.

Now that you have everything arranged for your first shadowing experience, having the right mindset is needed to make the experience a success. A day or two prior to your shift, spend a few minutes reflecting on what the ideal experience would look like to you. Envision how you will feel during and after the exercise. In addition, take some time to reflect on how you will show up to the shift. Coming in distracted or with a know-it-all attitude will guarantee that both you and the employee you work with will not get much value out of the experience. If you are going to invest a significant amount of time walking in your employees' shoes, you want to ensure that you approach the exercise in a way that sets you up for maximum value. Coming in with a grateful and empathetic approach, seeking to understand, and listening with intention provides you and the employees you work alongside the best opportunity to optimize the value of this experience.

Personally, prior to starting the shadowing exercise or while walking to the department on the day of the exercise, I would thank God for the opportunity for the experience and would visualize what success would look like at the end of my shift. I asked God to open my eyes to see what was needed to be seen and to help me treat the employees with the respect and humility they deserved. I prayed for help to not let my insecurities, fears, and defensiveness regarding what was not working trigger my ego or trigger the less-than-ideal leadership traits that would prevent me from getting the most from the experience. In addition, I prayed that God would help me build rapport with the employees I interacted with so they would feel comfortable to truthfully share their opinions and provide feedback about what areas of improvement they felt I should focus on. I prayed that I would be in the right mindset to receive the feedback, regardless of how it was packaged or framed, with the attitude of listening without judgment or defensiveness. I would always end my prayer with the request to help me learn the changes that were needed in order to make a difference (and alleviate any suffering) to the employees and the customers they served. I appreciate that not everyone has religious or spiritual beliefs, and in the spirit of transparency wanted to share with you my personal approach to my walking-in-my-employees'-shoes practice. Spending a few moments prior to starting your shift to reflect on your intentions and visualize how you want to show up as that ideal version of your best senior leader self while incorporating the sentiments above, will prepare you to be in the right mindset as you begin walking in your employees' shoes. Find what approach works best for you to help you prepare for this exercise.

## Asking the Right Questions and Learning to Listen

In addition to having the right mindset, asking the right questions will be helpful in optimizing the shadowing experience. Framing questions positively helps elicit feedback that will be most helpful for your understanding of where opportunities for improvement exist. Questions such as, "What is working well for you? What do you like about your current role? How do you feel you provide value to your clients to the department/team?" are all good questions to ask. Questions such as, "What are the one or two things that we need to stop doing or do more of?" work well to identify potential areas to free up capacity. Taking the opportunity to shift your employees into a more positive mindset as we did in Chapter 4 by asking, "What does the ideal working environment look like for you? What does the ideal client experience look and feel like to you?" will help your employees envision what is possible. These suggested questions are designed to help lead you to the following two questions I recommend you ask during your walking-in-your-employees'-shoes experience.

> "What is the one thing I can do to make your experience at work better for you?"

This one question will help you immediately cut through the fray of improvement opportunities to focus on what will make the most difference to your employee. The second question is similar.

> "What is the one thing I can do to make things better for our customers?"

Both questions identify the one thing, according to your employees, that will move the needle for both the employee and customer experience. This information will be utilized in Chapter 9, "Action that Moves the Needle."

Even better than asking questions is to simply listen and mirror back what you hear. Mirroring back the last few words an employee says will help elicit further information from them, which will be useful for you to better understand how they feel. If you are not familiar with this technique, try it at home with friends or with people you have just met. Simply repeat the last few words of what the person tells you, with a tone of genuine interest and curiosity, and then stay silent. Wait for their answer, listen to their response, and repeat. After those types of interactions, people will walk away knowing that you cared and were interested in them, their perspective, and their opinion. Furthermore, you want your employees to feel comfortable with this experience, because it may be rare that they get an opportunity to interact with a senior leader. Going into those interactions arrogant or defensive will squander any chance for your employees to feel that they were heard.

## Empathy to Build Rapport and to Build Trust

Empathy means understanding another person's perspective. It does not mean their perspective is right or wrong—it is what is true for that person at that moment in time. Empathy builds rapport with people and eventually builds trust. Leaders who have been afraid or uncomfortable with interacting with employees on the front lines because they are not sure what they will hear, or who are uncomfortable with being confronted with negative feedback, should step back and understand that all feedback is a gift. Understand that employee feedback is their perspective, neither right nor wrong. Do not judge it, but listen, reflect back what you hear, and seek to understand further by mirroring.

If you are ever confronted with negative feedback or anger, simply reflecting back what you observe to that employee will help reduce that negativity and will help them think about how they feel. Letting them know that you sense they are angry, unhappy, suspicious, or distrusting will help minimize those emotions. Reacting to their emotion in a way that does not empathize with them or appears defensive will only escalate the negativity, anger, or suspicion toward you and your intentions. Overcoming these negative emotions by seeking to understand is the key to work through these difficult confrontations with the positive outcome of better relationships and the beginning of building trust. Removing any preconceived notions you may have is important as you do this work. All employees, even the ones who are angry, bitter, and unhappy have reasons for the feelings they have (right or wrong). Seeking to understand and being curious as to the reason for their negative feelings, as opposed to being defensive or trying to justify why things are the way they are, will help you learn the reasons behind their emotions while building rapport and eventually trust with your employees.

At times, we, as leaders, feel the need to prove how competent, educated, and interesting we are to those we lead to justify our senior role or our salaries. Trying to prove your expertise during these walking experiences will alienate employees from you and will prevent you from building rapport and trust with them. As a result, you will miss out on learning the valuable perspective of those you serve.

## Rolling up Your Sleeves and Pitching In

Senior leaders rarely have the opportunity to roll up their sleeves and pitch-in when frontline employees are short-staffed or in a crisis situation. If those opportunities occur and you can help, by all means do so. The respect you will receive from your employees when you help during those times is immeasurable. If you need to help by answering phones, delivering supplies, carrying equipment, or providing customers with information or directions, when the time is right and help is needed, take advantage of the opportunity. Your learning will be incredible and the comradery and team-building invaluable.

Giving your leaders the permission and encouragement to jump in and help their employees by asking them what they can do to help has the same effect. Your managers will gain insight into the working conditions of their employees and will see where changes need to occur. Their employees will respect them in a new way. Yes, you may need your manager to attend a meeting you scheduled; however, giving them the permission to not attend that meeting so they can help their employees work through a busy stretch will be far more impactful than the outcome of your meeting, which can usually be rescheduled anyway.

## Connecting the Dots: Why Employees' Work Matters to Your Organization

Employees all want to know why their work matters to the organization and what they do on a daily basis provides value. While walking in the shoes of my employees, I would often take the time during that shift to connect those dots for them. If I was cleaning a patient bathroom with a hospital environmental service worker, I would explain how important their work was in preventing the spread of hospital-acquired infections to other patients. How impactful it was for the patient and their families that they did not get additional infections as a result of their hospital stay since our environmental team did such great work in properly cleaning their hospital room. I would also let them know how meaningful their interactions were to the patients they came into contact with on a daily basis. With our longer-stay patients, our environmental service workers would often take the extra time to chat with them, connecting with them in a way that bolstered the patient's spirit, which was especially meaningful to patients who did not have family in town to visit with them.

I did not really appreciate how important taking the time to connect these dots of how an employee's work specifically mattered to our organization and to our patients until one day when I was walking in the shoes of another environmental services worker, Amy. We were cleaning a nursing station on a unit, which was not under my portfolio, when I personally experienced how our own employees can devalue their co-workers and the important work they do. I was working the 7:00 a.m. to 3:00 p.m. shift that day, and within my first half hour of cleaning the nurses' station on the unit, I clearly understood how it felt to be treated as if I (or the work I was doing) didn't matter. I was being treated as if I was invisible. I was wearing scrubs, not my usual business attire. As I cleaned beside Amy, we both said good morning to the unit aides and nurses who were working at the station we were cleaning. To my surprise and disappointment, none of the employees said hello back. Even worse, they turned and moved away from us and to the other side of the station. I could see the embarrassment in Amy's cheeks, and I smiled at her, knowing I would debrief with her at the right moment and carried on with cleaning the unit. It seemed that at any chance the unit aides or nurses could get, they would specifically huff or puff if we were in their way and excluded us from any of the social conversation they were engaged in.

Around 8:00 a.m., a nurse, who was also a union leader whom I knew well, started her shift and immediately recognized me. We said hello, and she asked what I was doing dressed in scrubs. I explained to her that I was walking in the shoes of the environmental services team that day for the purposes of getting a better understanding of their working conditions so I could make any necessary changes to help them do their best work. As she left to start her shift, I continued with cleaning the unit, and within twenty minutes, I could feel a dramatic shift with the rest of employees working that morning. The staff politely said hello to both Amy and me. They began engaging us in their conversations and helping us with our work. I knew then that the word had spread of who I was and what I was doing that day. I knew then that I had much more work to do with improving our workplace culture.

As soon as the opportunity presented itself, I spoke with Amy about what we had just experienced. I explained to her the importance and value of the work she did for our patients and how her work directly related to the mission of our organization. I then apologized that our workplace culture had not yet lived up to our expectations or values and offered up the actions I would undertake to improve how we treated each other going forward. I could tell how meaningful the debrief was to Amy and the rest of the environmental team when she shared our experience with them. Periodically over the next few years, I made it a point to find Amy and follow up to see if she felt the impact of the workplace initiatives we were working on, which fortunately she did!

Had I not walked in Amy's shoes that day, I would not have experienced for myself the devaluing treatment of our environmental services team. In addition to my clinical and corporate responsibilities as vice president, I was also the chief human resources officer, having the responsibility for our organization's workplace culture. Even though we had just begun to conduct employee engagement surveys with a specific focus on creating a positive workplace culture, it wasn't until I had personally experienced that devaluing treatment that I realized annual employee engagement surveys could not be the only tool senior leaders relied on to get a pulse on the conditions their employees work in. I also realized that day, the importance of real-time feedback and connecting the dots between the purpose of the work our employees do with the purpose and mission of our organization.

## Purpose and Inspiration Drives Productivity, Retention, and Engagement

Research conducted by Bain & Company in 2015 concluded that if satisfied employees are productive at an index level of a hundred percent, then engaged employees produce at 144 percent, with the surprising result that the productivity level of an employee who is truly inspired by the purpose of their organization is at 225 percent. When you are able to paint the picture for employees of how their work matters, how it makes a difference to your organization, and how they fit in to your organization's mission, they are more engaged, they take pride in their work, and as a result, they are more productive. Today, more than ever, one of the most important drivers of engagement and retention is for employees to bring meaning to their work by understanding the contributions they are making for their organization.

## Capturing the Feedback

These next few steps are somewhat self-explanatory. When shadowing or working alongside your employees, you will want to capture the answers to any questions you asked, document your observations, capture items to investigate, flag issues or items that need follow-up, and record necessary changes. For me, the old-fashioned notepad and pen worked adequately. Dictating into the notes app on your smartphone will also do the trick. Whatever works for you will do the job.

Prior to ending your shift, make sure to loop back with the employee who trained and onboarded you to your shift and let them know how grateful you are for the experience and his contribution to your organization. Communicate your feedback about the experience and what your plans are to act upon the information gathered during your experience.

Circling back about your experience in a timely way with the director/manager of the department is critical. Most likely, your leaders will be anxiously waiting to hear how your experience went. In addition, they may be nervous about what their employees may have said about their leadership style and will want to be ensured you are not judging or reacting specifically to what was said.

If you communicated to your team and introduced the concept of walking in your employees' shoes, circling back to those same individuals will be beneficial. Communicating how grateful you were for the experience, your observations of what was working well, and what your plans are to work on some of the priorities identified will be useful. If a broader communication strategy was used to introduce the idea, taking pictures of your experience with the employees you shadowed (with consent, of course) to put in a newsletter or post online will help spread the message that you are interested in better understanding what you can do as a senior leader to improve the conditions of your employees so they can do their best work.

## Thanking the Employee and the Department

Depending on the nature of the shadowing experience, in addition to writing a thank you note to the employee I worked alongside, I would personally buy the department food as a way to say thank you for allowing me to spend a shift with their team. I would like to say that the food choices aligned with a healthy workplace philosophy; however, most times, it was donuts or beloved specialty baked goods from a local bakery. At times, I also included a gift card or a small gift for the employee to express my gratitude. The small gift or food is not necessary; it is your choice what is a fit for your leadership style and for the dynamics of the organization you work in.

## Prioritization of Improvement Ideas to Investigate, Better Understand, and Implement

After you have walked in the shoes of your employees, you will most likely have pages of notes, observations, and follow-up items to analyze. In a previous chapter, we worked on identifying time in your calendar dedicated to improving employee retention and engagement indicators. During this time you blocked off, focus on what priorities you want to work on, knowing that you can't fix everything overnight. Depending on how you crafted your questions and what you experienced, usually the top three priorities will be clear. If there are some quick wins that are easy to do, get them done and make sure to close the loop by communicating with the appropriate leaders and employees.

As you walk in your employees' shoes, avoid jumping to any conclusions regarding what you see and hear. Your observations and feedback from employees about what is not working well is just that—observations and feedback. Seeking to better understand what you hear and observe is critical, as opposed to having a "ready, fire, aim" reaction by making decisions that are not fully informed. Create a strategy to gather additional information and feedback about what you hear and see prior to making any rushed decisions. We will dive further into implementation of improvement opportunities in a later chapter.

## Walking in the Shoes of Your Employees and Employee Engagement

We began this chapter with the understanding that, as a senior leader, you have the opportunity to drive employee engagement through your leadership team, policies, the culture you create, and the expectations you set for your teams and organization. Additionally, you can personally drive employee engagement through your visibility and accessibility to your employees. Walking in the shoes of your employees provides you, a senior leader, an Incredible opportunity to personally engage with your employees by building bridges and relationships. Creating value as a result of listening, honoring, and connecting with them by understanding and improving their working conditions so they can do their best work. All the while, taking the opportunity in real time to connect the dots of why their work matters to your organization's purpose and mission. All of these are important elements of employee engagement that you can personally impact. I know this chapter is a firehose of information to take-in and process. I can promise you that having the faith to humble yourself and walk in the shoes of those you serve will be a game-changer, if not a life-transforming experience for you as well as your team!

## ———— Key Takeaways from Chapter 7 ————

- Understand the benefits of walking in the shoes of/ shadowing your employees.
- Understand the best approach to walking in the shoes of those you serve. This is not an exercise in spying or in trying to catch employees breaking rules or pro-

cedures but an exercise in better understanding their working conditions and building rapport and trust.

- Communicate, in advance, about your intention regarding the walking-in-your-employees'-shoes exercise.
- Have the right mindset and set intention around what you will pay attention to; this will help you get the most value from the exercise.
- Ask the right questions.
- Listen and reflect back what you heard with the mindset of seeking to understand more.
- Acknowledge the emotions of those you interact with and seek to understand the reasons for those emotions.
- Understand that empathy builds rapport, which eventually builds trust.
- Notice and reinforce the positive moments in your interactions, taking the opportunity in real time to connect the dots of how the employee's job specifically contributes to your organization's mission and success.
- Capture the feedback you hear.
- Thank the employees you worked with.
- Communicate your observations and any actions you will be taking to the relevant stakeholders.

**Chapter 8:**

# The Power of an Employee Engagement Team to Transform Culture

*"All employees have an innate desire to contribute to*
*something bigger than themselves."*

**— Jag Randhawa**

After reading the previous chapters, you may be thinking, "What? There's still more to do to solve my employee retention and engagement problem?"

We have spent the previous chapters building the foundation of an overarching employee engagement strategy—formulating the building blocks to recognizing you have a costly retention and engagement problem to solve, understanding why your employees are leaving or are disengaged, realizing your work as a senior leader is to connect with your employees by experiencing their reality by walking in their shoes, and creating a positive mindset of gratitude. These are all essential in providing a solid foundation for the remaining work ahead. Building up from the foundation we established are other strategies that will help you further connect with your employees, hear their voices, and build trust, which is essential to increasing employee engagement and employee retention.

In this chapter, we will work through one of the many surprises of my career—the power of an employee engagement team to lead cultural renewal in an organization.

Early in my career, I was blessed to be hired as a senior leader with the responsibilities of mission, organizational development, quality, and risk management at a midsize, acute care hospital. One of the responsibilities of my position was to oversee the reward and recognition committee. This committee did not have any employees, and it had a handful of somewhat-motivated leaders, who voiced their displeasure at the lack of effectiveness of the committee during the first meeting I attended. The committee had loose oversight for recognition events, including a successful "recognition of service" banquet coordinated by Human Resources. Other than that function, there was little else happening, except for the coordination of social events. Over time, this committee had evolved, more or less, into a social committee, mostly responsible for organizing events, such as the staff BBQ, golf tournaments, and ice-skating parties. Social events are important to an organization; however, it was consuming the time and energy of the reward and recognition committee to the detriment of any other work the committee could have been accomplishing.

After a few months of the committee exploring the possibility of rewarding employees who had low sick days each quarter (which we later found out was potentially discriminatory from a disability perspective), our new CEO, Phil, had asked if he could attend one of our meetings. During that meeting, after listening to the lackluster activities of our group, Phil asked one of the most important questions of my career. We were reviewing our committee's terms of reference, and when we reached the goals and objectives section of our terms of reference, Phil asked, "Why couldn't one of our goals be to become a Top 100 Employer?"

You should understand that, at the time, our organization was struggling and had been struggling for years. Our hospital was in a deficit position, and senior leadership was more concerned about turf wars than the frontline staff. Moreover, our culture was far removed from the culture of a Top 100 Employer designated organization.

The silence in the room was overwhelming. As the new senior leader responsible for mission and values, with the functional responsibility of the committee, I knew it was my place to respond to Phil's question. I knew if I agreed to list "achieving Top 100 Employer designation" as one of the goals, I would be responsible for ensuring this happened, which seemed like an impossible task. On the other hand, if I did not agree with the goal . . . well . . . you could imagine my dilemma. After what seemed like an eternity of silence, I took a deep breath, made the leap, and said, "Yes, why not? Why couldn't we become a Top 100 Employer organization?"

I am sure I didn't sound nearly as confident as I hoped, yet something shifted for me, for the rewards and recognition committee, for Phil, and most importantly, for our organization as I said yes. That shift was us moving from the mindset of what is not possible to what is possible. That was the day the stake was put in the ground, and we began working toward becoming a Top 100 Employer—a designation we eventually achieved two years in a row. It was also the day I understood the power of having a possibility mindset.

I wish I could say it was as easy as creating the goal to achieve the Top 100 Employer designation, and with a snap of the fingers, a year later, we achieved it, but it was not that easy. In hindsight, it was also not arduous either. It was almost effortless in the sense that we just started incorporating the goal of achieving the Top 100 Employer designation in most of the things we did. With the mindset that it was possible to achieve a Top 100 Employer designation and with the stated goal of achieving a Top 100 Employer designation, the necessary work to move us in that direction seemed to happen almost intuitively.

A few months later, I applied for and was promoted to vice president and chief human resources officer. This was a position that included an operations portfolio along with the chief human resources officer responsibility. In addition to my previous responsibilities of oversight for mission, vision, and values, I was now the chief human resources officer. I now had the additional responsibility for clinical and corporate teams and the fun responsibility of strategic planning all within my portfolio.

Based on employee feedback during my inaugural strategic planning retreat, the board identified becoming a people-centered organization as one of our strategic directions. As a result, becoming a Top 100 Employer designated organization was identified as one of our people-centered goals. Formally identifying becoming a people-centered organization as a strategic direction set the tone from the board of our organization to our employees that our organization's people were important—important enough to incorporate the audacious goal of achieving Top 100 Employer status!

I wish I could convey to you how far-fetched this goal seemed to be for all of us (including the board). By the time our board-approved strategic plan was rolled out, the excitement felt by our rewards and recognition committee (and me!) started to create momentum and an unstoppable movement was born. The power of having the mindset that anything was possible was pervasive throughout all the layers in our organization. It was felt not only at the grassroots level, but also by the board, our senior leaders, and the leadership team.

As an operational goal for supporting the "becoming a people-centered organization" strategic priority, the rewards and recognition committee transitioned into an employee-based and eventually an employee-led council. This was an important transition, as it was a signal to the employees that we wanted to hear their voices and that what they said mattered. We wanted to be clear that decisions were based on their input. In addition, the scope of the council expanded beyond just rewards and recognition tasks to a council that sought the voices of employees in our engagement strategies and in the areas that directly impacted them.

At the time the employee engagement council was created, our organization had not conducted an employee engagement survey. They had however, conducted a staff satisfaction survey a few years earlier, which provided clear evidence that staff were "not satisfied." I remember being handed a large, thick book during my first week on the job and being informed that the issues were mine to fix. It was difficult reading the results and the comments from the staff, even though I was not personally tied to the feedback since I was new to the organization. The cry for help from staff was evident and the heaviness of their feelings about the organizational culture was heartbreaking.

With our new strategic plan rolled out, we embarked on conducting an employee engagement survey. The new employee engagement council provided oversight of the implementation of the survey. They provided key feedback and direction to the administration of the survey, including communicating to employees, guaranteeing employee responses would be confidential, ensuring there would be no retribution for providing feedback, and designing employee focus groups to share the results, prioritizing the areas of focus and identifying actions to take. In addition, the employee engagement council thoughtfully and deliberately decided we would include the results (good or bad) of the soon-to-be executed employee engagement survey in the Top 100 Employer application package (which was optional). Our employees understood that if our organization was going to achieve a Top 100 Employer designation, it would be done based on what our employees said about our organization and not based on how good our application for the designation was.

These important decisions were made by employees who were members of the employee engagement council. Without their feedback, perhaps management would have made different decisions that would have unknowingly kept us on the previous cultural trajectory. As the executive sponsor for "people," I was responsible for providing support to the council, freeing up resources, removing any obstacles, building the initial momentum of the council, ensuring employees were available to attend meetings, being comfortable providing feedback, and developing a solid strategy to communicate the work the employee engagement council did.

In addition to a senior leader participating on the employee engagement council, the council's activities were reported periodically to our senior leadership council. This signaled that our employee engagement council and our employees were important to our senior leaders. More importantly, senior leaders were interested in hearing what employees had to say. This also signaled that we wanted to involve employees in decision-making (which I will discuss further in the following chapter) and that we could remove any barriers to progress and provide resources as needed.

At the beginning, recruiting the inaugural set of employees to become members of the employee engagement council was surprisingly challenging. We faced obstacles such as finding employees who were comfortable with participating and providing genuine feedback with management in the room and freeing them from their work responsibilities. This meant departments initially worked short-staffed or additional staff was brought in to replace them—easier said than done. Nonetheless, we were able to find a few brave employees and union leaders to become members. Over time, we approached individuals who were vocal about what they saw as organizational issues, and we tried to get them involved on the council to use their voices productively. When we started to include these individuals on our council, with guidance, coaching, and facilitation, some of our biggest naysayers turned into our biggest champions.

The value of the employee engagement council to lead employee engagement at our organization was critical to achieving our Top 100 Employer status, to achieving high employee engagement scores, and the key to changing the way our organization thought of employees in our decision-making processes. The employee engagement council was especially helpful as our organization worked its way out of a deficit position. Achieving a balanced budget at our hospital meant service changes, as well as employee changes. As senior leaders, it was *how* we began to make those difficult decisions, knowing that our strategic priority was our "people," which helped us to utilize the wisdom of our employee engagement council to think differently about our approach. In addition to that, the employee engagement council helped bridge the disconnect of our leaders from the reality of the front lines. During our meetings, management would periodically repeat stories they heard from other leaders. These stories would become the "reality" as they were repeated from meeting to meeting, rarely being "fact-checked" by the reality of what employees experienced or felt on the front lines. Employees felt safe at the employee engagement council to respectfully challenge these management mythologies for the purpose of becoming a better organization and improving the working conditions of the employees.

The composition of our council evolved over time and generally included equal representation from clinical, allied health, non-clinical/support staff, and management. Our employees told us they wanted fair representation across the different spectrum of employees, as opposed to only representation from one group (i.e., nurses). Management was also represented and did not exceed over fifty percent of the members of the council. In addition, we set term limits for committee members, chairs/vice-chairs were nominated, and we had a call for employee representatives. We asked employees in their expression of interest to be a member of the council to explain why they were interested in participating. The terms of reference below denote the overall responsibilities of the committee, which varied over the years and generally included:

- Oversight of employee engagement survey (timing, design, and implementation)

- Oversight of focus group sessions to help prioritize the action items as a result of the survey
- Implementation of action plans
- Communication strategy of the employee engagement survey—its results, action plan development, and status of the implementation of action plans
- Reward and recognition strategies (corporate and departmental)
- The introduction and oversight of the annual performance rewards based on individuals and teams who exemplified our mission
- Organizational development activities, such as training and development, professional growth of employees, and leadership development
- Wellness/healthy workplace initiatives

Our employee engagement council eventually evolved to review key HR performance indicators and included the oversight of our Top 100 Employer application. In addition, our council also vetted policies that impacted employees (such as dress code) for the purpose of getting and incorporating employee feedback. As the council evolved, our employees made the decision to separate out any discussion pertaining to social events and created an independent social committee for that purpose. Social committee activity could consume a large portion of the employee engagement council's time and the employees felt that it should be a separate and distinct committee to ensure both functions could get the dedicated time and energy they deserved.

An initial concern our managers raised as we began to include employees on the council was that it would become a place for employees to complain about their managers or air their grievances.

As a result, we laid out the ground rules in advance as to what the responsibilities of the employee engagement council were. In addition, we created rules of engagement for the council, which laid out how we spoke to each other respectfully and thoughtfully, listened with the intent to seek to understand (not judge), and were open to hearing others' perspectives. As the initial chair of our inaugural employee engagement council, I was able to gently redirect any employee-specific complaints about managers, compensation, or grievances to the proper channels for resolution. Over time, as the employees began to understand the purpose of the employee engagement council and their roles on the council, there was less need to redirect any issues that did not align with our mandate.

As the employee engagement council continued to evolve, the council became responsible for their branding and bi-directional communication strategy, which I will discuss further in Chapter Ten. At the end of each meeting, there was a standing agenda item—identifying key messages to communicate to employees. The employee engagement council then identified any key messages it wanted communicated to the employees and identified the most important item the council had accomplished during that meeting, both of which were included in our communiqué.

Having this standing agenda item ensured the voices of the employee were incorporated into our key messages since employee representatives on the council knew employees would want to know about our accomplishments and the work that would impact them in their roles. Once "communication to our employees" was a standing agenda item at the end of our meetings, our communication gradually became more effective, impactful, and meaningful.

Over time, our employee engagement council fully embraced and took ownership of the steerage of the strategic direction of becoming a people-centered organization. Our council members were proud to see how their work positively impacted our key people indicators, such as improved employee retention, increased employee engagement, and reduced absenteeism. The employee engagement council eventually became a place where all levels and sectors of our organization could come together for the common purpose of creating a people-centered organization, knowing the positive impact this powerful employee-driven council had on our employee experience and organizational performance!

## Positive Mindset—A Useful Tool for our Employee Engagement Council

Establishing a positive mindset—a mindset of growth, where all is possible—was as important to the members of the employee engagement council as it was for you in Chapter 4. Taking your employee engagement council members through a gratitude exercise where they identify what they are thankful for in their roles, departments, and organization will help shift their mindsets to positive ones and prepare them for the visualization exercise ahead. Asking your employees to then visualize what their ideal workplaces would look like in detail and having them individually write down what comes to their minds will help them think about and understand what is possible. Depending on the dynamics of your employee engagement council, you could then ask them to voluntarily share their visions for the purposes of creating a shared vision. Investing this time in creating positive mindsets and visions of what they can create helps set the groundwork that all is possible. This also identifies and removes limiting beliefs and encourages the idea that the members of the council are stewards, improving the quality of work life for their peers. This is incredibly helpful to get everyone aligned, working toward that shared vision, understanding that anything is possible. Starting and ending all employee engagement council meetings with these mind-setting exercises is also valuable to help create the conditions for the work, feedback, and decision-making ahead.

The momentum and evolution of our employee engagement council was incredible. As I sit here writing about the power an employee-based engagement council can have on an organization, I am looking at a signed "becoming a people-centered organization" t-shirt the council created with our logo and signatures from all the team members. I get goosebumps looking at this t-shirt, remembering the excitement, engagement, and enthusiasm of those employees.

That day when we first learned that our organization achieved what we first thought was not possible, a Top 100 Employer designation, was unbelievable. We held a celebration announcement in our cafeteria for all of our employees who made achieving the Top 100 Employer designation possible. Given the magnitude of the accomplishment, Phil, our CEO, and the board held a press conference, as this designation was significant to the community our organization served. Had Phil not had the all-is-possible mindset, had he not asked that question about becoming a Top 100 Employer years earlier, and had I not shifted my mindset (along with that of the rest of our committee's members) from what was not possible to what was possible, we would not have achieved the Top 100 Employer designation. More importantly, we would not have achieved all the cultural assets of increased retention and engagement that came with becoming a people-centered organization.

The Top 100 Employer designation was wonderful; however, the real accomplishments were the cultural tenets—the people-centric values, behaviors, and habits—that became instilled in our organization, our board, our leaders, and our people as a result of Phil's question. It was the transformation of our organization into one that truly valued its people that was so meaningful to us. The Top 100 Employer designation was validation that we had become the people-centered organization we'd hoped to achieve. Creating an employee engagement council was a critical element of our organization's transformation. Without it, management would have continued trying to do its best, implementing people-based strategies without the involvement of our employees, which would have missed the mark with respect to improving the culture and our key human resource and performance indicators of our organization.

## Key Takeaways from Chapter 8

- It is important to have a possibility mindset. Knowing all that is possible, as opposed to what is not possible, sets the direction and provides momentum in an organization.
- Creating an employee council helps build an organization that values the engagement of their employees.
- The employee engagement council helped bridge the disconnect between management and leaders (and the stories leaders repeat).
- Ensure that the employee engagement council has employees who are represented across your organization, with less than fifty percent coming from management, and include a senior leader representative.

- The employee engagement council should periodically report to senior leaders so they can support the work of the council, remove any barriers to progress, and provide resources as needed.
- Internal communication and the employee engagement council's branding are important to ensure employees are aware that the council exists and understand its purpose.
- The employee engagement council should include in their internal communications, key messages designed specifically for employees by employees, using the questions, "What would employees want to know about the work the council is doing?" and "How does it impact employees and their work environment?" as guides to frame the messaging.

## Chapter 9:

# Action that Moves the Needle

*"Don't mistake thinking for action and don't mistake
action for results."*

**— Orrin Woodward**

Within forty-eight hours of starting my new position as vice president, I realized how significant the cultural challenges and operational issues were of this large organization. As a result of decisions made by past senior leaders, the trust of their employees and the customers they served had eroded. I quickly understood the seriousness and gravity of these issues. During the next two years, I would be responsible for helping an appointed advisor address these concerns in order to strengthen our organization's culture.

Within the first few days, reports of cultural challenges were brought to my attention that initially, I couldn't believe were true. This information demonstrated the lack of respect and trust between the internal stakeholders of this organization, senior leadership, and the board. Several times during that week, I thought about submitting my resignation and getting as far away as possible. Not one to run from challenges, I managed to put my fear aside and continue with the orientation into my new role.

As part of my orientation, I had the luxury of meeting with the consultant who had conducted a culture assessment of the organization on behalf of the CEO. After the completion of the assessment, the CEO then hired him to implement his own recommendations and assume the interim vice president of human resources role. I was thrilled to be able to meet with this "expert" in the field and learn about all the actions he was implementing to renew the culture of our broken organization. Unfortunately, I quickly learned that even though he was implementing many action items, these actions were not even remotely aligned with the deep cultural renewal needs of the organization. Moreover, he demanded his whole leadership team stop working on their other initiatives so they could focus only on implementing his recommended actions. Sadly, this would never move the needle on healing the damage or the hurt of what the employees were experiencing, nor begin to repair the trust or restore the broken relationships.

Instead, the cultural renewal actions this "expert" was demanding from his leaders created further public drama. This eroded any last remains of confidence in senior leadership. When meeting with this consultant, he proudly shared all of the actions he had the directors and managers implement. He had everyone working twelve to fourteen hours per day, with no understanding of the incredible damage those actions were causing the employees. I, once again, was in a position to observe how the disconnect of senior leadership to the reality of the front lines can create more harm than good. Despite the countless hours the management team spent working to implement the actions the disconnected senior leadership team had ordered, not only did the actions not move the needle toward cultural renewal, they moved the needle in the completely opposite direction.

In this chapter, I will help you understand how to identify the actions needed to achieve the results you are looking for. In addition, I will review how you can work with your leaders to ensure they have the capacity to implement the actions identified to move the needle on employee engagement.

As leaders, we are all busy attending meetings, putting out fires, and responding to the never-ending emails and texts we receive. Phone calls, drop-ins, and even walks down the hallway to the bathroom typically result in issues to investigate and resolve. We are always busy doing something; however, is "that something" contributing to our ideal vision of senior leadership or organizational goals? Often, we do not think about what we are doing and how it contributes to our goals and vision. We just do the work that lands on our desk and move on to the next tasks. To move forward and achieve your goals of employee connection, engagement, and retention, you will need to act with that end purpose in mind. Being clear about your priorities is critical to expanding the capacity in your schedule, workload, and energy to dedicate to not only these goals but your other organizational goals as well.

In reading countless leadership books, articles, and blogs and attending many leadership courses, workshops, and seminars over the years, I found myself frustrated with the generic or academic advice provided. In addition, I have worked with big-firm consultants who would come in with promises of increased employee engagement and operational success. These consultants conducted surveys, performed assessments, compiled results, analyzed data, and produced comprehensive reports, identifying recommendations to implement. After the report was presented to senior leadership, the consultants who made those promises ended their assignment, collected the remainder of their consultancy fees, and left. Six months later, many of the recommendations had never been implemented as they lacked our organizational context. Their report collected dust on a bookshelf largely because the consultants typically fashioned their cookie cutter reports and recommendations from a template. As a result, the needle had not moved on the metrics we had initially engaged the consultants to assist with.

As mentioned earlier in the chapter, the consultant who was hired to implement his own recommendations used a heavy-handed approach to implementation and accountability, not understanding how those actions were going to impact staff. Although he understood the concepts of action, accountability, and how to check off the completed items in his project management spreadsheet, he did not understand whether those actions were the right ones to take at that particular time to drive the cultural change he had been hired to assess. Holding leaders accountable for actions not truly aligned with the needs of the organization is the equivalent of holding them accountable, as the overused saying goes, to rearrange the deck chairs on the Titanic.

Over the years, many studies across many organizations have come to the same conclusion: Move the needle on employee engagement and you move the needle on your organization's performance. Identifying action that moves the needle on employee engagement will not only help you achieve your retention goals, according to the research covered in the previous chapters (and in my personal experience), it will help you increase productivity, customer satisfaction, and profitability.

## Identifying Actions That Move the Needle

In the past few chapters, I identified many sources of information that will help inform your decision about what action you can take to move the needle on your employee engagement and retention scores. In Chapters Four and Five, you collected and reviewed information from some, or all, of the following: exit interviews, stay interviews, satisfaction or engagement surveys, and pulse surveys. In Chapter 7, as you embarked on the walking-in-your-employees'-shoes and shadowing experiences, you hopefully observed and heard many improvement opportunities. Some will be quick fixes or easy wins, and others will be more difficult to tackle. In addition, by asking two questions during your walking-in-your-employees'-shoes experience ("What is the one thing I can do to make your experience at work better for you?" and "What is the one thing I can do to make things better for our customers?"), you would have heard the single most important feedback from your employees to improve both your employee and customer experience.

## Employee Engagement Survey Action-Planning

Many organizations make the mistake of believing that conducting an employee engagement survey automatically equates to employee engagement. When done well, the survey process provides critical insights that can identify actions to take to improve engagement, retention, and performance. When done poorly, meaning no action taken, the wrong action taken, or action implemented in a non-valuing way, it can further erode the trust between the organization and its employees, resulting in disengagement.

Depending on the current state of your organization's approach to employee engagement, you may be starting from ground zero, having never surveyed your employees, or your organization has routinely conducted employee engagement surveys for years. Know that wherever you are on your employee engagement journey is okay, it is what it is. You are on a path to take the next steps needed to further improve your employee experience. If your organization has not conducted surveys previously, there are numerous employee engagement survey providers, consultants and software platforms to help you measure employee engagement.

If your organization has conducted employee engagement surveys, utilized consultants to assist with interpreting the results, but have not seen the needle move on engagement, understanding why is crucial. In some organizations, senior leaders or human resources will hire consultants to fix their employee engagement issues and will let them do all the work. Often, this leads to numerous power point presentations and/or employee engagement programs that don't impact engagement. If that is the case for your organization, identifying if your senior leadership team truly owns employee engagement and not delegating it to consultants or human resources is a good place to start to see where corrections might need to be made.

I will not dive deep into the statistical analysis needed to ensure your organization isn't just taking your results at face value. There are plenty of organizations that specialize in this work. Generally, when reviewing your data, looking at particular cross-sections of responses, key driver analyses, and your results from specific employee segments. These will help you identify underlying issues within your organization, and subsequently create actions, which will move the needle on engagement, performance, and productivity.

If your senior leadership team has not reviewed your most recent employee engagement survey results from a strategic perspective to identify the organizational actions to undertake, I would recommend that as a first step. When reviewing this information, the temptation is to try to tackle everything or to delegate action planning only to managers. This leads to disjointed plans, which aren't then fully implemented. Having senior leaders review the results at a high-level and create an organizational action strategy is crucial. Surveying employees and not taking any organizational action will further erode the trust in senior leaders, resulting in no improvement or decreased engagement. As a senior leader, I understand the challenges that arise in an organization. You roll out the results, you get busy, other priorities come up, and before you know it, it's time to resurvey your employees without many of the actions identified implemented. Building in a plan to take action, with resources assigned to support implementation *before* the survey is deployed, is critical to ensure there is organizational capacity to implement the actions.

When building an organizational action plan to address your employee engagement results, it is crucial you don't fall into the trap of trying to address it all. As a senior leadership team coming to consensus, prioritizing three to five items that are most important and are feasible to accomplish will help ensure that you're not biting off more than you can chew.

As a next step, once your organization action plan is created, review your portfolio results with your leaders, keeping in mind your managers are most likely anxious about the results and your reaction to their departmental scores. Each department's results will vary, depending on the nature of the work, classification of employees, and their team culture. Meeting with your departmental leaders individually for the purposes of discussing their results will help you better understand the unique dynamics and challenges within each of your leader's teams.

According to Quantum Workplace's research, "Employees who said managers followed up with them post survey were twelve times more engaged than those who said their managers did not follow up. Worse yet, employees who said their managers didn't follow up experienced a six-point decrease in an overall engagement score from the previous year." Holding management-facilitated employee focus groups to review the survey information and identify actions that move the needle on employee engagement will inherently increase employee engagement.

Providing your leaders with the tools they need to hold action-planning sessions is critical. Most managers were promoted to their positions due to their technical strengths and have not had training in the leadership essentials of facilitation, active listening, and understanding what drives employee engagement. Include in your manager toolkit and training, the outline for their meetings with employees, including an overview of what employee engagement is. In addition, provide key messages for managers to convey to their employees as to why employee engagement is important to them as a manager; why it is important to your organization; what the purposes of action-planning is; and that the employees' role is to help identify actions that will improve their engagement. Having your managers facilitate open discussion with their employees to brainstorm and identify (and agree to) two or three actions of improvement to work on is itself an engagement driver as it demonstrates to your employees that their voices have been heard and their opinions count. In addition, follow up from the manager at future team meetings on the progress of the implementation of the action-items further demonstrates commitment to engagement.

## Action Planning for the Rest of Your Data

Since not all organizations are in the same place with respect to measuring employee engagement, the above recommendations may not be a fit for your current situation. In addition, you may have collected data from exit interviews and your walking-in-the-shoes-of-your-employees' experiences for which you want to build actions of improvement. As with the employee engagement surveys, including your employees in the discussion to identify two or three items to work on is key to drive engagement. For the intention of consensus building and identifying opportunities for improvement to focus on, take the themes that emerged from exit interviews and the answers to the one-thing-I-can-do questions and hold employee focus groups. Employee focus groups help you gather deeper insights into employee engagement. In addition, it will help generate actions to address the trends and themes from the information you collected and prioritize what actions to take to improve the environment for your employees. This manager-facilitated process of having employees prioritize the top actions to make their experience at work better for them helps employees feel valued and heard. It also demonstrates to them that managers are interested in improving the conditions so they can do their best work for their customers, helping to ensure you are taking action that will move the needle on employee engagement and, as a bonus, customer satisfaction.

To facilitate these employee focus groups, you can either hire a third-party resource to assist you with this exercise, utilize your Human Resources or organizational development departments for this work, conduct the focus groups yourself, or utilize the leaders within your team. Another option is to utilize an online survey tool, such as SurveyMonkey (free for its basic version), as a way to ask your employees to prioritize which actions would have the most impact on improving their and their customers' experiences. In the previous chapter, I spoke about the creation of an employee engagement council; this council can also be utilized to help prioritize which three to five actions you and your leadership team should focus your time and energy on.

If your recommendations are department-specific, you can quickly get the pulse from your employees at a departmental or team meeting about what they believe the priorities are. Using the basic, "You get three dots. Place them on what priority, or priorities, are most important to you" strategy is a quick and easy way to identify the top two to three actions that employees would like you to focus on that will move the needle on employee engagement.

As with conducting employee engagement surveys, if you are not serious about implementing or making change, do not ask your employees for feedback about actions you will never implement. Nothing will disengage employees quicker than asking for feedback about actions to improve their working environment and then being unwilling to implement them. I get it! There are some things that can't change or you are unwilling to change in an organization. If that is the case, don't ask your employees their feedback about those items, and instead, focus on the areas in which you are willing to implement change.

## Setting the Appropriate Timeframe

Setting an appropriate timeframe for this work is crucial. If your timeframe is too short for non-easy fixes, or non-quick-win items, you will not achieve the implementation goals. This will disappoint your employees and quickly demonstrate to them you are not serious about creating change or implementing feedback. Any trust you started to garner by asking for their feedback will quickly erode. If you have too long of a timeframe to implement changes or opportunities for improvement feedback, employees will lose faith that you are working on improvement changes. The momentum you built by walking in your employees' shoes, administering surveys, and holding focus groups will also be lost. To avoid losing momentum, identify an appropriate timeframe that allows you the capacity to truly implement the improvement opportunity. That balance can be tricky; however, working with your leaders to see what capacity they have and helping them see their work through the priority lenses of employee connection, engagement, and retention will help them focus on what they can let go of.

## Helping Leaders Implement the Action That Moves the Needle

Based on your employee feedback, you have identified the actions that will move the needle on employee engagement for your leadership team to work on in an appropriate time frame. Next, set up an accountability framework that is mutually agreed upon by yourself, leader(s), and, if appropriate, the person or board you report to. Utilizing project planning software or other tools to help with identifying tasks, goals, responsible party (or parties), and deadlines for implementation of the actions identified by your employees to increase engagement will be useful.

In a world that collects copious amounts of data, which our leaders have to access, it is no wonder leaders get lost in the sea of analysis paralysis. As a result, any action, let alone the right action, is rarely implemented. Taking the time as a senior leader to help your leaders identify what actions they are responsible for and helping them find the capacity and the mindset for this important work is where you can provide incredible value.

As you work with your leadership team in assigning responsibility and accountability for the implementation of these action items, permission is key. Your leaders work hard. Understanding that the work they are doing is aligned with your priority and goals of moving the needle on employee engagement is necessary so that your team is firing on all cylinders in an effort to achieve those goals. Helping your leaders understand what they can let go of and giving them permission to stop or pause some of their busywork so they can dedicate their time and energy to the important work (implementing change that best helps your employees' working conditions and best helps them improve their customer experience) is critical.

Once your accountability framework to implement the actions identified by employees to move the needle on employee engagement is in place, hold weekly leadership meetings or huddles (you can do this daily, if it is a high-priority and critical safety item) to discuss the status of the work necessary to complete the implementation of the action items. As a senior leader, your role is to see what obstacles you can assist in removing for your leaders. In addition, you are providing permission for your leaders to stop working on other items that may arise that are not aligned with your priorities. As is the life for a leader, just because you identified moving the needle on employee engagement as your key priority, this does not mean the rest of the fire-fighting work disappears. Your role as a senior leader is to help your leadership team navigate these fires and provide clarity around the other busywork that arrives so your leaders know what they should be prioritizing. By letting your leaders know what they can let go of, pause, or stop altogether, ensures their efforts are focused on actions that move the needle on increasing employee engagement.

A side note here on providing permission as a senior leader to your leadership team: I use the term "permission," not in its autocratic definition, such as "you need my permission before you make a decision," but in the aspect of letting your leaders know that it's okay to not do something. Managers tend to think they need to do everything on their plates to satisfy their direct supervisor and often need direction or, as I have phrased it, permission, let go of activities and work, which are not aligned with the priorities you have identified.

## Creating a Positive Mindset to Move the Needle

As has been the theme in the previous chapters, checking in on your mindset is essential. Purposeful action does not occur without taking the time to ensure you and your leaders have a positive mindset to embark on implementing the actions that will move the needle on employee engagement. Mindsets controlled by the limiting beliefs of, "there is too much work to do; these identified improvement opportunities are impossible to implement; or there is not enough time in the day to get everything done," are mindsets and phrases you or your leaders may naturally be saying or thinking. This thought process, however, compounded with vocalizing these statements aloud, is a mindset of what is *not* possible. If you think and say these limiting beliefs, that there is not enough time and the identified opportunities are impossible to implement, then guess what? There will not be enough time and those opportunities for improvement will not be implemented. With a mindset of what *is* possible, you have the capacity to focus your efforts on the work to implement the actions and help move the needle to improve your employee engagement and retention metrics. With a possibility positive mindset, you create the space in your mind that it is possible and with this mindset, you fulfill your destiny.

## Attention and Intention

Now more than ever, today's world is full of distractions. As senior leaders, this is especially true for us. The distractions of social media, texts, phone calls, the 24-hour news cycle, sports scores, and blogs can quickly move us off the tasks we intend to do. Additionally, we are inundated with data, analytics, best practices, and marketing from our competitors, such that we are at risk of being pulled off course by the next shiny new thing we see in a slick custom-designed marketing ad. Attention with intention is essential to keep us aligned with our goals.

Through the earlier chapters, you have shaped your intentions with understanding *why* employee retention is important and *what* your ideal senior leader self looks like when at your best. Paying attention to your thoughts, words, and actions will help you know if they are aligned with the intentions you set. As the T. Harv Eker saying goes, "Where attention goes, energy flows and results show."

As in previous chapters, take the time to shift back into a positive mindset for yourself. Think about what you are grateful for and go back in your mind to the exercise in Chapter 4, reminding yourself of your vision of your ideal senior leader self. Reflect on *your why* employee retention and employee engagement are important to you and imagine what the ideal conditions are for your employees to do their best work. Taking the time to do these visioning exercises will help you shift your mindset to implement the actions needed to move the needle on employee engagement. Depending on the relationship you have with your leaders and how comfortable you are with the positive mindset philosophy, you may choose to provide your leaders with these tools and introduce them to these gratitude and visioning practices. Providing your leaders with the understanding of these positive mindset tools will help everyone achieve anything you set your minds to!

In addition to helping your leaders establish a positive mindset, creating an environment for your leaders that gives them permission to take risks without fear of reprisal, judgment, or humiliation is just as essential as is understanding your leaders' strengths and potential. Helping your leaders see that they can do the work ahead, instilling a sense of confidence in them, motivates and garners their commitment to taking the action necessary to move the needle on employee engagement.

## Employee Engagement—A Continuous Journey

In Chapter 6, you carved out time in your schedule for the purpose of employee engagement and retention. You can utilize this time to review the progress you and your leaders are making toward the implementation of the actions your employees identified to move the needle. Continue to scrutinize your calendar on a daily basis, or even several times throughout the day. Routinely ask yourself if the meetings you attend provide value in moving the needle on employee engagement or retention. This exercise will help you better understand where there is additional time and capacity. Continuously scrutinizing your calendar to align how you spend your day and energy through the lens of your priorities of employee connection, engagement, and retention is essential. Remember, this is *the* work to do.

Employee engagement is a continuous journey, one of the most important practices to implement is to begin and end your day with the questions, "How can I be of service to my leaders and employees today" and "How did I provide value to those I serve today?" Most days, plenty of things will come to mind as to how you provided value to those you serve. Ending your day with the acknowledgment and gratitude for the opportunity to be of service provides you with some evidence that you are making a difference and personally contributing to moving the needle. If, by chance, your day was one of *those* days that went off the rails, and you cannot identify many times where you felt you provided value, that is okay, too. We all have those days. Take the time now, without judging yourself, to re-evaluate what busywork or non-productive, nonessential meetings pulled you away from your ideal senior leader self and prevented you from providing the value you know you can. Know that tomorrow is a new day, and you can make different decisions about how to spend your time so that you can provide value to those you serve.

As you implement the actions your employees identified as the priorities that will make their work experience better for them so they can do their best work for the customers they serve, you will see the needle move on the key engagement and retention indicators you reviewed in Chapter 4. In addition, as employee engagement increases and your employees choose to stay with your team and organization, based on the research outlined in the previous chapters and in my personal experience, you will also begin to see the needle move on your organizational goals of improving the customer experience and profitability. As employee engagement is always a work in progress, you will continue to evolve your engagement practices to get a continuous pulse on how your employees perceive their work experience. In the chapters ahead, I will walk through additional strategies to assist in creating a culture where employees feel valued, knowing they have the opportunity to do their best work for the customers they serve.

─────────  **Key Takeaways from Chapter 9**  ─────────

- You realized that even though you and your leaders' schedules are at capacity, after evaluation, you might find it is often "busy" work, which is not aligned with your priorities.
- Analysis paralysis and the role of data mining, collection, and analysis can lead to inaction.
- Not all action is the right action to move the needle.
- Taking no action could result in no improvement or decreased engagement.
- Senior leaders need to own employee engagement with their leaders.
- It is important to build a high-level organizational action plan to address the priority areas where improvement is needed.
- You can utilize tools such as departmental meetings, surveys, focus groups, and employee councils to help identify which two to five opportunities (depending on your capacity) for improvement will have the most impact on employee engagement and retention.
- Assigning and holding your leaders accountable for tasks without understanding what is on your leaders' plates or what capacity they have to do the work will not only disengage your leaders and burn them out but will also allow for little probability that the needle will move on your employee engagement/retention indicators.

- Provide a safe environment for your leaders, giving them permission to stop and pause items they are working on, which are not aligned with your priorities.
- Take the time to ensure you and your leaders have the "all that is possible" mindset as you approach the improvement opportunities.
- With your leadership team, mutually create an accountability framework, as opposed to assigning tasks to leaders with timelines that may or may not work.
- Scrutinize your calendar and workload to ensure how you spend your time aligns with your employee engagement priorities.
- Assist your leaders in scrutinizing their calendars and workload to ensure how they are spending their time aligns with the priorities of employee engagement.
- At the end of the day, ask yourself how you provided value to those you serve.
- Identifying the right actions to implement to move the needle on employee engagement, and ultimately productivity, will help you achieve your departmental goals and organization's strategy.
- The power of paying attention to your intention will keep you focused on taking the actions needed to move the needle.

## Chapter 10:

# Creating a Bi-Directional Communication Strategy

*"Internal communication isn't about telling employees what to think; it's about creating and enabling authentic, ongoing dialogues with and between them."*

**— Paul Barton, ABC**

f I had to bet money on the most common theme that emerges from employee engagement surveys, I would bet it is communication, specifically bi-directional communication. Communication to, with, and from employees is one of the critical cornerstones of any employee engagement strategy. You could invest all of your time into employee engagement initiatives and also work on opportunities for improvement as suggested by employees; however, if they are not aware of the changes you made based on their feedback, then it might as well not have happened at all.

You understand communication is important, and you feel that you spend a lot of time communicating *to* employees. But that is just it—*you* are communicating *to* employees. You might not even be actually communicating; you might just be passing along information. Bi-directional communication is a two-way dialogue between you and your employees. Employees don't want to be talked at or talked to; they want to be engaged in a conversation about all that impacts their world.

According to Towers Watson, companies with highly effective communication practices enjoy forty-seven percent higher total returns to shareholders compared to organizations with poor communication. In addition, many studies have identified that communicating effectively internally is linked to higher engagement of employees. As a result, more organizations are focusing on understanding how effective their internal communication strategies are.

As a senior leader, while designing your internal communications strategy, you need to take into account the drivers of employee engagement. Crafting your messages with the awareness that employees want to be heard, valued, and informed is crucial. They want to understand why and how organizational decisions are made. In addition, your employees also want to have input into the decisions that impact them before the decisions are finalized.

I appreciate the recent shift in leadership thought that attributes employees wanting to better understand what their employer is doing and why they make the decisions they do. This could be, perhaps, the vocalized expectations of the younger millennial generation as opposed to the non-vocalized approach of the baby boomer generation. Baby boomers had jobs for life and a pension if they just did the work and didn't ask questions. I have a bit of a different perspective. Regardless of age, I see bi-directional communication as a basic and fundamental need that all people have. Perhaps the millennial workforce has made it more common for employees to request or demand open communication. At the end of the day, everyone wants to be heard, valued, and informed. Whether it is expectations from younger generations or the fact that employees no longer have the golden handcuffs of pensions and are more mobile to move to a different organization if they feel the grass is greener, organizations are now in the position to explain their decisions to their employees if they want to retain them and create an engaged employee culture.

In my experience, effective communication—whether organization-wide, department-specific, horizontal, or vertical— was a continuous challenge and journey of improvement in most, if not all, of the organizations in which I worked. I hate to say it, but earlier in my career, I did my best to delegate the communication of employee engagement strategies to the "communications department (or team)." In my mind, since the communications team is generally responsible for the creation and distribution of newsletters, coordinating town halls, and hosting the intranet and Internet, it made sense to me that they would "own" employee communication, as well.

After a few years of trial and error in working with the communications team to develop key messages and identify the appropriate vehicles to effectively communicate the great work we were doing, I realized that I, the leadership team, and the employee engagement council had to also take responsibility for communicating our messages to ensure they were heard by employees. When all of us had ownership of bi-directional communication (and not just the communications team), our bi-directional communication strategy and effectiveness was much more robust and effective. I will spend a considerable amount of time in the next chapter discussing how to get employee input as part of your bi-directional communication strategy. In this chapter, I will focus on how to approach communicating with your employees to support employee engagement, retention, and performance.

## The Standard Tools

Most organizations have standard corporate tools for organizational communication. These can all be effective vehicles of communication, depending on the message, the audience, the importance of the communication, and the time-sensitivity of the message. Most likely, you have an internal communication strategy in place. It is essential to assess your strategy to ensure it is delivering on your employee engagement and retention goals. I have listed a few, but not nearly all, of the communication tools and vehicles:

- Employee newsletters
- Attachment to paystubs (if still using paper) or embedded statements on e-copies
- Employee intranet or internal "members/employees" only website
- Notices in lunchrooms, bulletin boards
- Memos or communiqués
- Letters to employees
- Group emails or texts
- Departmental meetings
- One-on-one discussions

- Townhalls
- Employee huddles
- Employee "suggestion box"
- Messages required to be read when an employee logs in
- E-learning modules
- Slack
- Departmental communication boards
- Social media
- Video messages
- Online conferencing
- Chat rooms

There is no shortage of internal communication vehicles for organizations to utilize to communicate their key messages. Identifying your internal communication channels and understanding if they are effective and delivering the right message to the right audience is important. You also want to know how these vehicles enhance the employee experience. Conduct a review of your communication vehicles and assess if they support transparent communication, connecting employees to your organization, initiatives, organizational values, strategy, and goals—all of which are significant drivers of employee engagement.

## Dependency on Email as a Communication Tool

When we asked our employees what vehicles were best to communicate information to them, we were surprised with their responses. What employees thought were effective communication tools looked very different from what management thought was effective. For example, at one organization where I worked, our management and communications team felt that email was the best means to communicate information organizationally. As a result, we embarked on the costly initiative to provide all two thousand employees with an email address to access organizational communication. After a six-month implementation process that provided an email address for each employee and provided computer stations in central areas for employees to access their emails, we were surprised that there was not much improvement with the uptake of key organizational messages. *After* the implementation, we asked our employees why they were not reading the emails or were not receiving the "important" messages we communicated. Our employees provided us with the feedback that email had become the "go-to" strategy by everyone to communicate. Employees (if they had time) had to log into their accounts (if they could successfully remember their passwords) and were inundated with emails from anyone and everyone. Consequentially they did not know which emails were important. Emails regarding social events, fundraising events, non-essential information, and time-sensitive information were sitting unopened in our employees' inboxes.

In addition, employees did not have time built into their workdays to read emails or online newsletters . . . and certainly not the time to respond to them. Building in the thirty minutes of time to process emails would mean adding additional employees. Yes, emails may (or may not) be an effective tool for leaders or salaried employees who do not have production targets to achieve or services to provide. Our employees who had patients to serve, supplies to deliver, and rooms to clean did not have time to read the countless emails waiting for them in their inboxes. Hmm . . . if perhaps we had only asked our employees for input in advance of spending significant dollars to implement our initiative, which ultimately did not achieve our desired communication outcome, we could have repurposed those dollars for other, more effective strategies.

As an effort to regroup on our internal communications strategy, realizing it was not the silver bullet our leaders had thought it would be, we debriefed with our employees. We asked them how we could deliver key messages to them in a timely and effective way. What worked for the employees in this organization was communication through daily or twice-a-week huddles with their leaders. Huddles are brief, scheduled consistently, built into the employees' workflow, and provide in-person two-way communication regarding pertinent information.

Having their direct supervisor or manager prepared with the key, succinct organizational soundbites allowed for employees to hear the *important-to-them* information in real-time and, most importantly, allowed them the opportunity to ask questions and provide feedback. In addition, the employees suggested utilizing or creating departmental communication boards, posters, screensavers, and cafeteria table tents as tools to get our messages delivered to those who did not have the opportunity to check email, who worked infrequently, or who worked different shifts. While these communication vehicles may not be a fit for your organization, the take home message here is to ask your employees what works best for them.

Studies show employees feel their organization's communication strategy is failing as critical information gets lost. Mapping out your approach to internal communication strategically with your current tools can address information overload.

If your organization's internal communication design and structure expects employees to read emails and e-newsletters, it is essential they are designed in a way to be read on the go with a smartphone. Keeping your content more bite-sized and shorter will help employees who don't have the time to read long messages digest the information quickly. If you are currently tracking open and click rates on your newsletters, it would be worth validating your assumption that your employees have read the communiqué and absorbed the information. Incorporating read time metrics may help you understand the full story about your employees' uptake of the information you are sending them. Again, holding employee focus groups for the purposes of understanding what they feel are effective internal communication tools is essential to knowing that your key messages are being read and understood.

## Communicating with Multiple Generations

With multiple generations working together in an organization, communicating effectively in a style that reaches all generations is the next frontier of internal communications. Surveying your employees to better understand their communication preferences so that you can design a system with multiple communication channels is how organizations need to evolve with cross-generational employees working in their organization. Everything from emails and videos calls to staff apps and gamification to how you hold townhalls, need to be evaluated through the lens of all generations in your organization. What worked a decade ago may not be effective for your younger employees, and what works for your younger employees may not be a fit for the baby boomers. In addition, each successive generation has demanded more transparency, feedback, and collaboration with their employers. It is essential that your internal communication strategy is aligned with these expectations. Taking the time and resources necessary to move people to the platforms that work best for internal messaging is needed to ensure all your employees can participate in your bi-directional communications strategy.

Capturing the wisdom and knowledge of seasoned employees and building in opportunities of mentorship with their younger peers, helps boost performance of both employee groups. Allowing for and encouraging open dialogue between the baby boomer employees and millennials is beneficial as it breaks down the generational walls that might exist.

## What about the Messaging?

When employees are informed, they make better decisions— decisions that impact their productivity, and most importantly, the customers they serve. The days of top-down, regulated, tell-employees-only-what-we-think-they-should-know communication from senior leaders as an organization's only internal communication strategy is quickly coming to an end. Knowing there are plenty of vehicles in which to communicate your message, we now need to focus on the questions, "What is the message?" and "How do we craft it in a way that drives employee engagement?"

After years of trial and error and continuously asking our employees the question of what they valued in regard to communication, we realized that the basics of "why, what, where, who, and how" is what we needed to incorporate into all of our messaging. Employees want open and transparent communication. They want to know why and how decisions are made and what those decisions mean specifically to them. Linking your internal communications messages with how an employee's work is connected to your strategies helps employees understand why their work matters. Incorporating what you want the employees to do with this information, while preparing the messaging, helps you create organizational action. Generally, if employees understand the reason behind what you are asking them to do or about a decision that was made, they are more inclined to give their support.

We also heard from our employees that our messages need to be written in a way that employees can understand. Employees on the front lines may not necessarily understand the boardroom or senior leadership lingo we use in all of our meetings. Taking time to know our audience and craft our messages in a way that resonated with our employees was important feedback that only they could have provided us.

Logos, simple graphics, and charts are tools that can help capture messages that may otherwise be tuned out, not heard, or not retained. In one of the organizations where I worked, we used graphics to capture the essence of the strategic directions of that organization. We issued our communiqués, notices, memos, and anything we could with the logo of the corresponding strategic direction. This helped ensure the subject matter of the communication tool was tied to a specific strategic direction. This was a win-win for helping immerse the strategic directions into our organization.

Regardless of the methods of internal communication your organization uses, periodically holding employee focus groups to see how you can continuously improve the effectiveness of your communications and messaging is essential.

## Trust in Leadership Through Transparency

Trust in leadership is another key employee engagement driver, which is linked to organizational success and growth. Trust is strongly connected to consistent organizational transparency. Leaders openly sharing information—the good and the bad— and not hiding problems, even when difficult, helps build the foundation of trust that employees crave. A Harvard Business

Review 2013 employee engagement survey revealed that seventy percent of those surveyed said they are most engaged when senior leadership continually updates and communicates their organization's strategy. As a senior leader, your role is to provide consistent communication regarding your organization's strategy. Review your message through the lens of building trust by asking if your message is truthful, respectful, and accurate, as opposed to sugarcoating the situation you are trying to communicate. Communicating less over email and becoming more visible by providing your updates in person or through video interaction will help employees become more personally engaged with you as a senior leader. Additionally, consistently aligning your actions with your words is how you, as a senior leader, can model the way for your leadership team and employees.

## When to Share Messaging

As a new senior leader in a past organization, I learned a fundamental communication tip from the communications director—always tell the employees first. Tell employees before you tell anyone else about changes, whether good or bad. The communications director repeated this sentiment endlessly. The last place you want employees to hear of organization change, good or bad, is from the media, social media, or through the grapevine. You want your employees to trust you as a leader, and nothing breaks that trust quicker than hearing about a crisis event, breaking news, or organizational changes from the news, social media, or worse yet, the rumor mill. I understand this is a difficult task in the fast-paced world of social media, yet this is paramount for organizational culture and trust. Utilizing instant information communication tools, such as employee communications apps, is one way to help immediately inform employees about changes before they read about them from an external source.

## High Touch versus High Tech

At one point in my experience, it reached the point where our managers used email as the only mechanism to communicate to their employees, and these same employees did not have the time to access emails. Email had quickly replaced face-to-face communication. In addition, the intranet became the one and only place where corporate communication occurred. As a result, we had to take a step back and re-evaluate our internal communication strategies.

## High Touch

Emails, Slack, the intranet, and other technology solutions are helpful and should be utilized selectively, thoughtfully, and with purpose. What did we do when these technology tools were not available? How did we communicate with our employees in the world without technology? When we asked our leaders and employees how they would like to receive communication, rarely a technology solution was identified as a preference. Topping the list were "just tell me" and "just ask me." Our employees preferred face-to-face communication over trying to find the time to access a computer to attempt to find the pertinent email out of all the emails in their inbox. Humans, by design, are social beings who desire relationships and desire to be part of a larger community. Face-to-face conversations with leaders help facilitate the feeling of community. In addition, it allows for two-way communication that drives engagement. Technology certainly can play an advantageous role with internal communications, but it can never replace the benefits of face-to-face communication.

## High Tech

We have the great fortune to be living in a time where advances in technology allow organizations a plethora of solutions to bridge the communication gaps that working remotely and across multiple organizations in multiple countries and time zones bring.

While millennials and Generation Z are becoming more of the workforce and expect social media and apps to be a part of an organization's internal communication vehicles, less tech savvy generations resist technology. Finding technology solutions that provide multiple channels that address the needs of all generational preferences is essential for internal communications to be effective. In addition, understanding how to identify the right technology to integrate at the right time for the purposes of employee engagement is the challenge many organizations are facing as they contemplate the ROI of bringing in an internal collaboration platform that can effectively reach their employees anytime and anywhere. With the increase in these anytime-anywhere technology tools comes the risk of employees being connected to their work and always "on." Although these advances in technology may be effective in engaging employees with their ability to provide anytime access, employees quickly burn out with the expectation of always checking their devices and responding, which has the opposite impact on employee engagement from what you may have originally intended. Involving your employees to help you find the right balance between high-tech and high-touch internal communications tools for the purposes of driving employee engagement is paramount.

## Helping Our Leaders: Preparing Them as Facilitators

As with all employee engagement drivers, your leadership team plays a vital role with how they effectively communicate with their employees. Providing leaders with the tools and expectations of the role they play in engaging their employees in bi-directional communication is crucial to help increase employee engagement, decrease turnover, and achieve your organization's goals.

As a first step, build in the expectation of all leaders (including senior leaders) to engage in open and transparent communication with their employees. This includes the expectations of asking for feedback from employees on important issues, active listening, and helping employees connect the dots as to how their work impacts their departmental and organizational goals. Next, equip leaders with speaking points for organization-wide initiatives to use at their staff meetings. In addition, you can provide managers with specific questions regarding corporate initiatives to ask employees for the purposes of encouraging dialogue and gathering feedback. This was helpful to build our bi-directional communication strategy. Given these expectations, our managers had to fully understand the organizational initiatives prior to speaking with their employees and asking for their feedback. Consequently, our leaders' uptake of their knowledge of these organizational initiatives increased exponentially. Our leaders were pleasantly surprised by the productive and open discussion they had with employees when we provided our leaders with discussion questions to ask them. Requesting our leaders to ask their employees for feedback on organizational initiatives opened the door for them to have further discussions with their employees about departmental changes and updates.

Spend time with your leadership team to discuss how they can create an environment where employees are able to provide their honest opinions without fear of negative consequences or retribution. Teaching your leaders how to reflectively listen, without judgement, without becoming defensive, or without jumping to conclusions is essential to ensuring employees can share their opinions openly.

Senior leaders need to communicate effectively with the leadership team to ensure they are engaged, informed, and prepared to communicate effectively with their employees. In addition to asking leaders for feedback on organizational initiatives, connecting the dots for leaders as to how their role is connected to the organization's mission is essential. Creating a culture that encourages leaders to speak up and say what is so for them allows for a diversity of opinion that makes the leadership team stronger as a result. How you as a senior leader communicate with your leaders models the way for how your leaders communicate with their employees. Routinely, asking your leaders how you as a senior leader can communicate more effectively with them is also helpful.

## Mindset and Communication: How They Work Together

A key theme throughout these chapters is having the proper mindset while communicating, preparing the messages for communication, listening to your employees, and seeking to understand their feedback.

A key driver of employee engagement is employee voice. Most employee engagement surveys include a question that speaks to the issue of employees feeling heard, their opinions being valued, and feedback responded to. Listening is different than hearing your employees and waiting for your turn to respond. It helps you expand your understanding and is most effective when it is authentic.

### Authentic Listening

Authentic listening is when you give full attention to what your people are saying for the purposes of understanding their opinions, ideas, and feelings. As a senior leader, authentic listening is one of the most powerful ways you can create value. Authentic listening begins when you pay attention to your intention as you listen to your employees and leaders. Since seeking to understand employee feedback is a driver of employee engagement, setting your intention to be curious and open to all perspectives to better understand your employee's opinion will help you to focus on your employees' needs rather than on your own agenda. Listening with the intention of, "How can I help this employee?" enables you to focus your attention on not only what they are saying, but what they are not saying. As Peter Drucker once said, "The most important thing in communication is hearing what isn't said."

Although it may seem obvious, it is essential to understand that a negative mindset or mood has significant impact on how you communicate and interact with your leaders and employees. You can take the time to create a positive mindset prior to communicating with them. Additionally, you can remove any limiting beliefs, such as the idea that you do not have the time to dedicate to bi-directional communication or the time to ask for feedback from your employees.

In the previous chapters, you have seen a variety of ways to shift into a positive mindset, a mindset where you are open to hearing your employees' feedback and view that feedback as a gift. Having a mindset where you seek to better understand, not judge the feedback is an essential element to a bi-directional communication strategy. As in any relationship, bi-directional or two-way, communication is critical to strengthen your relationship, show your commitment, and build trust.

## Continuous Evaluation of Your Internal Communications Strategy

Regardless of the tools your organization uses to communicate with your employees, asking employees to continuously provide feedback on their effectiveness ensures your communication strategies are helping support your employee engagement goals. Moreover, just by asking for their feedback, it engages your employees in bi-directional communication. Another win-win!

The intent of this chapter is not to provide you with a one-size-fits-all internal communications strategy, rather provide you with a different perspective in which to view internal communications. In this rapidly changing world of technology, it's easy to get caught up in implementing the latest high-tech communication strategy, platform, or gadget to deliver pertinent information to your employees. Understand most of these high-tech solutions cannot replace what employees need most—to be really heard and engaged in authentic dialogues with their leaders.

Communication is the foundation of employee engagement and organizational success. Communicating consistently and effectively with your employees helps them understand their roles and how their work aligns with your strategic goals. Additionally, through effective and consistent communication, you will increase productivity, enhancing the competitiveness of your organization. As a senior leader, continuously paying attention to how you listen with the intention of seeking to understand your employees' perspective will help you create value, strengthen relationships, and build trust. These are essential contributors to employee engagement and retention. In the next chapter, we will further build on bi-directional communication by proactively engaging employees, asking for their feedback before decisions are finalized to ensure their voices are heard and their opinions count.

───────── **Key Takeaways from Chapter 10** ─────────

- Understand the differences between information sharing and bi-directional communication.
- Ask employees what effective communication looks like to them.
- Use communication as a tool of trust.
- Use messages that speak to the "why, what, where, who, and how" questions in your messaging.
- Include how the key messages relate to employees' work and what employees are to do with this information.
- Understand all leaders and teams own communication, not just the communications team.
- Recognize you may need multiple communication channels to accommodate the needs of multiple generations' communication preferences to be effective.
- Tell employees first, before they hear it from media, newspapers, or rumor mill.
- Equip your leaders to facilitate open and honest discussions.
- Know that when employees are informed, they make better decisions, and this impacts their productivity, and most importantly, the customers they serve.
- Create a positive mindset in approaching communication.
- Understand the importance of authentically listening to your employees.

## Chapter 11:

# Proactive Employee Engagement

*"The most effective way to cope with change is to help create it."*

**— L. W. Lynett**

After years of leadership development opportunities, conferences, workshops, and trips to India, one would have thought I had learned all that I could learn from a leadership perspective. And I thought I had until the day I learned what should have been an intuitive leadership skill: engage your employees in policy development and decisions that directly impact them before you implement the policy or make the decision. This sounds simple enough. Yes, it is simple, but is it easy? Not so much.

At the height of popularity for the Crocs shoe, my director of employee health and safety, Jennifer, informed me during a meeting that she was going to institute a "No Crocs" policy at our organization. In general, I supported Jennifer's decision. Crocs are the backless shoe with multiple holes on the top and sides, which did not adequately provide for the safety of our employees' feet from sharp objects and hazardous spills in the clinical environment. With my support, Jennifer went ahead and implemented the "No Crocs" policy across our organization. What I was not prepared for was the immense backlash and pushback from our employees.

One of the individuals who led the backlash against the "No Crocs" policy was Mary, an emergency room nurse practitioner and an informal leader, whom I (and many of her colleagues) respected immensely. After the policy was implemented, at the height of the backlash, Mary requested a meeting with me. During the meeting, Mary shared with me the frustration she and her peers had with the "No Crocs" policy. As I explained the safety concerns surrounding Crocs, Mary asked why we chose to single out Crocs specifically rather than creating a general safe footwear policy. Mary explained that Crocs had made a healthcare-specific shoe that addressed our safety concerns. As we had banned all Crocs from the workplace, she and other healthcare workers could not wear the healthcare-specific model of shoe.

Mary was also upset we implemented the "No Crocs" policy without consulting the employees. While Mary appreciated our perspective regarding safety concerns on most models of Crocs in the marketplace, she was rightfully upset that we did not consult with employees in the first place. If we had, we may have learned about the healthcare-specific model of the Croc shoe, which appeared to have addressed the safety concerns. Moreover, there were many Croc knockoffs, which were equally unsafe, ones we had not banned from the workplace. If we had asked our employees first, perhaps we would have taken a different approach with the development of the "No Crocs" policy and avoided the significant backlash we faced. I thanked Mary for her feedback and told her that I would speak with my director of employee safety and get back to her.

The conversation with Jennifer did not go as well as I had hoped. She did not want to hear about the healthcare-specific Croc and was adamant about keeping the "No Crocs" policy in place. In my experience, taking this kind of hard black or white stance never served the employees I led or me very well. My belief is that most issues that arise in leadership are not black and white. They tend to be grey, and our job as leaders is to resolve these tensions and conflicts through thoughtful consideration and deliberation of all perspectives. It is challenging for leaders to adopt a both/ and approach. Fortunately, in my experience, I am comfortable working in those grey, not-everything-is-black-or-white spaces. I usually find a middle ground and accomplish the overall goal while including others' feedback. I realized, as the leaders in this case, we had failed to do just that. By taking an aggressive position of "no Crocs" without consultation, even though the intention was right (employee safety), the approach was lacking and uninformed.

Realizing I was not getting anywhere with Jennifer, I asked her to outline the objective of the "No Crocs" policy. She said, "To keep our employees safe."

To this, I said, "Then we need to create a safe footwear policy that lays out the foundation and guidelines for shoes that our employees can wear that keep their feet safe in the workplace."

Yes, it was far easier in the short run to create and implement the "No Crocs" policy without exceptions. Allowing us, as leaders, to check off the box that we were protecting our employees.

However, with our strategic priority being a "people-centered organization" and keeping in mind that "asking our employees for their feedback" was one of our strategic goals, I knew we needed to correct our course. I asked Jennifer to take a step back and reevaluate the "No Crocs" policy and take into consideration the feedback from our employees. Although stepping back to reevaluate the "No Crocs" policy was a bit of a hit to our egos, we knew it was the right thing to do.

Over the next two weeks, Jennifer did the research on what was considered safe footwear in the clinical environment, and based on the evidence, she redrafted the "No Crocs" policy and turned it into a "Safe Footwear" policy. This policy included specific heel height, no open toes, no holes in the shoes, guidelines on the height of the back lip on the heel of a shoe, and ensuring the shoe was slip-resistant. This draft policy was then vetted with the employee safety committee, which included employee representatives. We invited Mary, who brought in a pair of the healthcare-specific Crocs to vet against the new policy. We then vetted the dimensions and specifications of the safe footwear policy and measured the Croc healthcare-model shoe to see if it would be compliant (which it was). The policy, with included revisions from employees, was then approved and subsequently implemented. Finally, the "No Crocs" policy drama and backlash was over!

Coincidentally, our quarterly leadership development day with our managers occurred during the time of the backlash and policy revisions. I used this event as a case study during the leadership day, since several of our leaders who were impacted by employee pushback (including Jennifer) were in attendance. As we broke down the event, one of the coaches helped us see the light of how much time, energy, and frustration (for both management and employees) could have been avoided if we had only asked our employees for their feedback in advance of implementing the "No Crocs" policy. By taking the approach we did, we demonstrated a lack of understanding about what was happening on the frontlines, resulting in feelings of resentment, disbelief, and distrust toward management. Had we sought feedback from our employees in advance, we would have learned about the healthcare model of Crocs and developed the appropriate policy based on feedback from our employees.

As we broke down our real-time case study, looking for the lessons learned, it was a significant "aha" moment for all of us— the demonstration of the importance of asking for feedback from our employees in advance of making decisions and implementing policies. Going forward, I used the lessons learned from our "No Crocs" policy blunder and applied them to the development of future policies and decisions that impacted employees. As a result, as an organization, we started to vet draft policies that impacted our employees with employees in advance. The most notable one was an overhaul of our dress-code policy that included sensitive discussion items, such as facial piercings, tattoos, and others. By vetting the proposed changes to our dress code in advance by way of an employee survey followed by employee focus groups, we were able to implement much-needed changes to piercing and tattoo coverage without employee pushback. We also achieved high employee compliance since we did the hard work of asking our employees for their feedback on a draft policy in advance of implementation. Yes, the concept of proactive employee engagement is a simple one, yet implementing this leadership principle feels harder and longer in the short-term. However, the saved time and preserved good relations as a result of taking the time to ask for your employees' feedback in advance of policy or decision finalization is worth it in the long run.

Having incorporated the lessons learned from the "No Crocs" policy into my leadership toolkit, I have implemented many difficult, controversial, and challenging policies that impacted physicians, unions, and employees . . . and did so without challenge or issues. In addition, I fostered trust, built better relationships, and understood the issues the policies covered in a much deeper way as a result of asking for feedback by the employees and stakeholders impacted in advance of implementing the policy.

## Proactive Employee Engagement as a Bi-Directional Communication Tool

In the previous chapter, I walked you through the benefits of bi-directional communication as a tool to drive employee engagement and largely focused on the vehicles and channels of information sharing. Asking employees for feedback is the other half of bi-directional communication. Understanding how best to approach incorporating employee feedback into your organization to optimize your employee experience is what I will address in this chapter.

As mentioned earlier, many organizations equate employee engagement with conducting an employee engagement survey. Other organizations may conduct employee engagement surveys and reactively implement actions to address areas of concern. Measuring employee engagement is a good reactive tool to help organizations know where to focus their efforts. Proactive employee engagement allows for organizations to engage employees outside of the annual survey process.

There are many ways to ask for employee feedback in advance of policy approvals and finalization of decisions. The first rule of thumb is that decisions and policies that have an impact on your employees should include employee feedback before decisions and policies become finalized. The second rule of thumb is that if you are not willing or able to include feedback from your employees in policies or in the decisions you make, don't ask them for feedback. As mentioned previously, there is nothing more discouraging and disheartening to employees than when we ask for feedback and don't listen to it. Of course, there are times when you are not able to include employee feedback into certain policies or decisions due to regulations or financial limitations within your organization. At those times, let your employees know that those are the reasons you are not able to ask or include feedback from them.

Once you identify what you will ask your employees for feedback about, you should identify the appropriate mechanism by which to do so. If it is a departmental process, policy, or decision, depending on the number of employees impacted and the shifts your employees work, you can ask for feedback at staff meetings, via a group messaging email/app, or you can ask for volunteers for a focus group in which the policy or process is reviewed. If you are looking for feedback on corporate policies or organizational decisions, then conducting a survey (using a survey tool like SurveyMonkey) and asking employees for their feedback on key areas of the policy is an effective tool. In addition, depending on the nature of the policy or decision and the importance and impact the decision or policy has on your employees, you may want to seek volunteers for a task or focus group to work through the results of the survey to help reach consensus regarding what to include in the policy or decision. As I discussed in Chapter 8, titled "The Power of an Employee Engagement Team to Transform Culture," this council is another vehicle you can utilize to vet your draft policies, or better yet, if an organization-wide policy impacting employees is needed, you can look to your employee council to draft it.

As a senior leader, when you are chairing or participating in any committees, build in the expectation that policies impacting employees come forward for your committee's approval and have had employee feedback. If these draft policies have not had employee feedback, send them back without approval until appropriate stakeholders, those groups the policy impacts, has vetted them.

As you collect employee feedback, and where possible, include it into decisions and draft policies that impact your employees, you will realize that not all of your employees' feedback can be incorporated. At those times, it is critical to communicate back with your employees, thanking them for their feedback, explaining what was included, why it was included, and how it shaped your decision-making and policy development.

## Other Ways to Proactively Engage Employees

In addition to proactively asking your employees for feedback regarding decisions and policies that have direct impact on them, developing an inventory of when or what initiatives into which you, as a senior leader, want to incorporate employee feedback is a helpful strategy. Doing so will ensure you are capturing feedback in all areas that would benefit both the employee experience and your organization. From collecting employee feedback to include in your strategic planning retreat to setting of goals and objectives, from understanding why indicators may be not achieving the intended target to assessing the effectiveness of communication strategies, and from determining what is meaningful recognition to how you celebrate as an organization, all organizational activity becomes more effective and robust as a result of asking and incorporating your employee feedback into these initiatives.

## Proactive Engagement of Employees as the Key to Successful Change Management

No leadership book would be complete without touching on the topic of change management. Although there are many resources available for successful change management adoption, I feel it is important to mention the critical aspect of change management that often gets dismissed: Involving employees is the key to change management. As the saying goes, "Do it *with* them, not *to* them." Employees want to feel empowered in finding the solutions your organization is looking to resolve. They also need the tools and support from their managers, along with a trusting culture, to garner the confidence that they can find the solutions and create change.

For successful change management to happen, employees from all levels of the organization need to be engaged in the design of the implementation strategy. As leaders engage those employees most impacted by the change, it will minimize resistance to the change (as those employees helped design the change) and increase adoption.

As you begin any large change initiative, even if you are working with a consultant group to help you manage the change, ensure the time and resources are budgeted and dedicated to involving employees in all aspects of the change. Employees need to be included in every aspect of the change to ensure buy-in and support of your initiatives. Set the expectations with your consultants that employees are included at the beginning to learn about the change, to design the change processes, and in the creation of the measurement systems used to determine if the change is succeeding or failing.

I appreciate that it may not be practical or possible to involve every employee in every decision. By asking your employees how to best get adequate representation in key decisions will help ensure your change management strategy is designed for success.

## The Managers' Role in Proactively Engaging Employees

As an organization, it's one thing to engage employees proactively in corporate initiatives, and it's another thing to ask your managers to do this with departmental changes, as well. As with all change management initiatives, employees will buy into decisions and policies better if they had a part in creating them. Convey to your managers that when they take the time to involve their employees in unit-level decisions that directly impact their employees, their employees will be less resistant to the changes being made or policies being implemented. Most importantly, the managers will save significant time by taking time on the front-end of policy development by involving the employees and hearing their feedback, as opposed to implementing changes blindly without understanding the employees' work environment and having to course-correct after the fact when employees resist the changes.

## Having the Right Mindset When Proactively Engaging Employees

The reality of leadership today is that leaders are busier now more than ever, with more demands asked of leaders than there is time to address them. Understanding the value of proactively engaging employees will help you to take the time needed to gather employee feedback and incorporate it. I know from personal experience that it may feel easier to lead from a place of command and control (our egos certainly like that approach) than it is to take the time at the front end by leading through engagement. The traditional hierarchal models of organizations and leadership may have their place and provide needed boundaries, but there is still room to proactively engage employees in advance within those boundaries. Approaching decision-making, policy development, and goal setting through the lens of proactive engagement of your employees helps build trust. This is accomplished by demonstrating, through your actions, that you value their feedback and are listening, all of which foster employee engagement and loyalty.

By now, you are familiar with the positive mind-setting exercises I have covered in the previous chapters. Identifying and working through your limiting beliefs, such as *there is not enough time to proactively engage employees in advance; there is too much to do to create additional steps to proactively ask employees their opinions; I already know what my employees are going to say, so why bother asking them for their feedback,* is an important step to shift into the positive mindset where all is possible. Foster a mindset that you do have enough time to proactively engage employees, valuing their feedback to not only make the best decisions possible but to also create the conditions for your employees to do their best work for the customers they serve.

If you are having trouble working through your limiting beliefs, spend the time shifting back into a positive mindset by thinking about how grateful you are to be in a position of service to those you lead or how grateful you are that you are in the position to provide value as a senior leader by creating the conditions based on employee feedback so they can do their best work. Visualize who you are as that ideal senior leader when you are at your best, reminding yourself about *your why* regarding employee engagement and retention.

As you continue to build in the practice of gratitude and visualization of your ideal senior leader self, coupled with your strong sense of why employee engagement and retention is important to you, you will move into the positive mindset of confidence in which you believe nothing is impossible. As you shift into this positive mindset of confidence, leaving your limiting beliefs behind, you can step forward, taking the necessary steps toward positive action to achieve your goals of creating the conditions for your employees to do their best work for the customers they serve.

Although asking for employee feedback in advance of making a decision or approving a policy seems like a basic and simple task, many leaders unfortunately and consistently don't take the time to seek the feedback. It feels cumbersome, time-consuming, and has the potential to open a Pandora's box of issues. However, when properly and consistently done, asking and incorporating employee feedback saves time in the long-run (less firefighting, compliance issues, and unhappy staff), garners buy-in, and builds trust and respect from your employees. Employees feel valued and their opinion is heard, which are all cornerstones of employee engagement and retention.

## ———— Key Takeaways from Chapter 11 ————

- Proactively engaging employees in advance of a policy or decision that impacts them helps you achieve your objective in a way that garners the employees' buy-in and aligns with their roles, while making employees feel their feedback is important.

- Identify the policies or decisions you make that impact employees, and if you are willing and able to incorporate their feedback, use an appropriate tool to ask for that feedback.

- Don't ask for feedback if you do not plan to include feedback into the policy or decision.

- You can include employees and feedback about decisions in advance by holding focus groups, using pulse surveys, and discussing them with them at departmental meetings or huddles.
- As policies come forward for approval at committee or executive meetings, it is important to ask whether employees were able to provide feedback about the policy prior to it landing at the senior leadership table. If not, have an organizational philosophy that, prior to approval, policies are vetted with employees.
- Communicate the outcome of the feedback process, letting your employees know what was included and why.
- The process takes longer in the short-term (having to ask and incorporate feedback on the front-end). However, the savings in time in the long run and the increase in staff satisfaction are worth it.
- Ensure that you have the proper mindset when approaching proactive engagement.
- Understand the managers' roles in proactive engagement.
- Proactive employee engagement is the key to successful change management.

# Chapter 12:

# Recognition and Beyond

*"People work for money but go the extra mile for recognition,*
*praise, and rewards."*

— **Dale Carnegie**

## Recognition to Engagement to Retention

Early in my career as a leader, I was asked to meet and greet employees at Christmas luncheons as a member of the senior leadership team. I showed up to my first luncheon and was asked to give each employee, on behalf of the organization, a small Christmas gift as a thank you. The gift, which included the name of our organization and cost a few dollars to produce, did not provide any practical value to our 1,300 employees. Our organization was in a significant deficit position at the time. We had recently issued layoff notices and planned to announce additional layoff notices in the New Year.

None of the employees who I handed the gift to appeared happy or appreciative about it. In fact, I heard rumblings about why management would spend money on useless swag when we didn't have money to buy the supplies we needed and were conducting layoffs. I also heard, "I just need a thank you from my supervisor, not a useless gift I won't ever use." Being a new member of the senior leadership team, I asked my colleagues why we would spend money on these gifts when we were in a deficit position when the gifts did not appear to be of value to the staff. As I conveyed my observations to the other senior leaders, they said, "This gift is how we show our appreciation." I looked around at the other senior leaders, wondering if they were trying to be funny, and to my surprise, they were serious. They genuinely thought the useless swag we gave away at the Christmas luncheons was appropriate recognition.

At that point, the disconnect of my colleagues from how our employees wanted and needed to be recognized was very clear. To the senior leadership team, the gift represented a checkmark in the box of recognizing our employees at Christmas, but to several employees, the gift was a token, disconnected attempt from leaders to say thank you, especially in the fiscally-challenged environment we were operating in. Instead of feeling valued, our employees felt slightly offended. This left our employees feeling little trust in the competency of their senior leaders. This two-dollar-per-employee investment from our organization did little to help retain our employees, let alone help them feel rewarded or engaged.

I share this story to illustrate that when senior leaders attempt recognition without connection to their employees, the recognition comes off as hollow, disconnected, and at times, devaluing—the opposite impact from what was intended. The intention may be good, but the execution leaves employees feeling unrecognized. In addition, our organization was spending money it really did not have in an attempt to recognize our employees at Christmas. If those dollars had be repurposed for something our employees valued and was tied to organizational performance, the leverage those same dollars could have had in both recognizing employees and positively reinforcing our organization's priorities would have been significant.

## Recognition—Creating Value as a Senior Leader

Several reasons motivated you to read this book. You wanted to solve your employee retention problem and create value as a senior leader. Based on the feedback from employees in numerous studies, the single most important way for you to create value and solve your retention problems is to provide honest, timely, authentic, and meaningful recognition of your employees. Concurrently working with your leadership team toward creating a culture of gratitude and employee recognition will help them retain their employees and provide value as well.

According to a Gallup post, titled "Employee Recognition: Low Cost, High Impact," Gallup's analysis indicates, "only one in three workers in the U.S. strongly agree that they received recognition or praise for doing good work in the past seven days. At any given company, it's not uncommon for employees to feel that their best efforts are routinely ignored. Further, employees who do not feel adequately recognized are twice as likely to say they'll quit in the next year." Gallup's analysis of workplace recognition also indicates that it "motivates, provides a sense of accomplishment and makes employees feel valued for their work. Recognition not only boosts individual employee engagement, but it also has been found to increase productivity and loyalty to the company, leading to higher retention." (Mann, Dvorak 2016)

Regardless of your personal approach to recognizing your leaders and employees, ensure you are creating a culture where employees feel valued and are recognized for their positive contributions. This is how you can directly provide value as a senior leader while impacting your engagement and retention scores.

## The Role of Manager with Recognition

When I started asking individuals at the employee engagement council how they felt about our corporate recognition initiatives, I heard interesting feedback. The main takeaway was that we could spend as much as we wanted on corporate recognition initiatives, but unless our employees felt recognized by their immediate supervisor or manager, the corporate initiatives would not make an impact. Our employees acknowledged that corporate recognition initiatives are important and needed. However, without direct supervisor/manager recognition and positive feedback done in a timely way, the corporate recognition initiatives would not make a difference.

We asked the members of the employee engagement council what their ideal vision of meaningful recognition from their supervisor and manager looked like. We were surprised that leading the list of suggestions was a simple *thank you.*

Employees wanted to hear, "Thank you for working late to clean a patient room after your shift ended so that another patient could be transferred from the emergency room to the floor. If you had left when your shift was over, it would have been another hour before that patient could have been transferred."

"Thank you for working through your break to help answer the patient's family's questions about their family member's care as they arrived."

"Thank you for assisting another team member with their assignment when they were behind with their work."

To our employees, a supervisor or manager seeing them go above and beyond in their roles by acknowledging it and genuinely thanking them, specifically and in real time, meant so much to them—much more than a token two-dollar swag gift from a nameless senior leader at Christmas. Our employees wanted specific and timely verbal feedback from their managers or supervisors. As a bonus, a hand-written thank you note would also be wonderful. Yes, our employees' suggestions about meaningful and valuable feedback were simple; yet, I knew the implementation and execution of this recognition strategy at a supervisor and manager level would not be so easy to implement.

In my experience, most leaders want to provide positive recognition to their employees. The challenge frontline leaders have in providing specific and timely feedback to their employees is their often-overloaded plates of work. This work, which may or may not be aligned with their organization's strategic priorities, was likely not an important priority of employee connection, retention, and engagement. Managers and supervisors who have employees that work three shifts, seven days a week have access challenges with seeing what their employees do. Furthermore, they do not have easy access to employees to provide timely feedback.

It is difficult enough for managers with employees working a typical Monday to Friday, 9:00 a.m. to 5:00 p.m. shift to physically see their day-shift employees, understand how they are positively contributing in their roles, and provide timely and valuable feedback, let alone try to do the same for their off-shift and weekend employees. Managers or supervisors are often occupied with meetings, training sessions, budget oversight, hiring interviews, staff onboarding, or the investigation of employee or customer complaints. These obligations take managers away from their important work, the important work of being visible and accessible to their employees on the front lines. Being available and visible to employees provides managers not only the opportunities for meaningful connection with their employees, it creates the conditions for the managers to recognize their employees in real-time when their employees go above and beyond. Employees who work off-shifts and weekends rarely see their direct manager or supervisor. If they do, it is usually to investigate a complaint or provide negative feedback and not to provide what employees crave—positive, specific, and timely recognition. So how do leaders bridge the gap?

Bridging the gap comes with building expectations for leaders to provide meaningful and timely recognition to their employees and making time to be accessible and visible to them. As a senior leader, helping your leaders understand this expectation and helping them navigate their responsibilities is essential. Giving leaders the confidence to say no to obligations that take them away from being visible and accessible to their employees, without fear of recourse, is your important work to help create a culture where employees feel valued and recognized for their positive contributions.

Asking your leaders routinely how and who they have recognized recently, helps convey to them that timely and meaningful recognition is important to you as a senior leader and an expectation you have of them. Connect the dots for your leadership team members regarding the importance of their roles in providing timely and authentic recognition of their employees.

Employee recognition is a key employee engagement driver that improves retention and ultimately customer satisfaction. Explaining this to your leaders keeps the larger picture in mind as they try to navigate their own priorities on a daily basis.

## Manager Recognition Strategies

As the saying goes, people leave managers, not companies. Much research over the last two decades has repeatedly proven the importance of timely, authentic, and specific recognition provided by their direct manager as a key driver of employee engagement and retention. While some organizations have implemented complex performance-based compensation reward packages for their employees, research has identified that "praise, attention from leaders, and opportunities to lead projects were more effective motivators than performance-based cash rewards, increase in base pay, or stock options." (McKinsey & Company).

There are many tactical strategies for managers to provide meaningful recognition at a departmental level. Understanding that frequent and authentic recognition, aligned with departmental goals and values, will not only help their employees feel valued, it will engage them and positively reinforce what it is the managers value from their employees. Some of these tactics include:

- Morning huddles: They are great opportunities to recognize employees in front of their peers and to ask employees who they observed acting in a way that aligned with the mission or values of an organization (a win-win, as well, to help reinforce the mission and values).
- Monthly face-to-face employee check-ins to provide positive feedback on work done well and to provide employees with the opportunity to provide feedback

regarding their work and what areas of improvement they observe.

- Recognize employees who go above and beyond by giving them the opportunity for informal leadership roles within the department.
- Provide employees who show initiative in specific areas the opportunity to participate in departmental task teams or organization-wide task teams.
- At departmental meetings and during one-on-one meetings, ask employees what meaningful recognition looks like for them.

It is important to note that although rewarding employees is a key driver for engagement, which in turn drives retention and organizational performance, recognizing employees who are not performing in a way that is aligned with the values and departmental goals could have the opposite impact on the top performers on their team.

## Recognition, Employee Engagement, and the Impact to the Bottom Line

Research conducted in 2012 by Josh Bersin found that recognition programs could have a huge impact on business performance. "Companies that scored in the top 20 percent for building a recognition-rich-culture, actually had 31 percent voluntary turnover rates!" In Josh Bersin's *Forbes* article, "New Research Unlocks the Secret of Employee Recognition," he stated, "Most CEOs would pay millions to reduce voluntary turnover, and it turns out that a well-designed recognition program can achieve this result." Additional research has found that recognition is a significant driver of employee engagement, which leads to greater customer satisfaction and an increase in profitability, ultimately having a positive impact on an organization's bottom line. According to Greg Barlomiejczuk in a 2015 Cornell University ILR School article, "Employee engagement has been shown to be a significant factor in improving a variety of organizational outcomes, such as customer loyalty, profitability, employee productivity, and retention. Employee recognition, in turn, has been found to positively relate to employee engagement, with one study suggesting that 41% of the variation of employee engagement is attributable to the strength of recognition an employee receives."

Even with plenty of research and evidence that both recognition and engagement of employees positively impacts the bottom line of organizations, senior leaders tend not to focus on recognizing employees, leaving it to the Human Resources team to do. As a senior leader looking to create value, personally taking ownership of the engagement and recognition of your employees by making it a priority will not only create a culture where employees are valued, it will help you achieve your organization's goals.

## Organization-Wide Recognition Initiatives

As a solid and timely direct supervisor recognition strategy is designed and implemented, a concurrent focus on organization-wide initiatives is needed for an all-encompassing approach to creating a culture where employees feel valued and recognized. Recognition should not be designed as a one-off program; it is a complete shift in mindset. Incorporating gratitude and recognition pervasively in your organization, and through multiple channels, will create a culture where employees feel valued. Often, organizations define their recognition strategy as the employee perks of Ping-Pong, foosball, dry cleaning pick-up, in-office massages, free food and nap pods. Many studies have found these perks, although nice to have, do nothing to move the retention and engagement needles to remain competitive in recruiting top talent.

There are many ways to incorporate recognition strategies throughout your organization. I will review some of the basics, as well as next level and beyond strategies for you to consider when assessing your organization's approach to recognizing your employees.

## The Basics

### Service Recognition Events

Most organizations have recognition strategies that include service-level recognition. In my experience, when designed well, these recognition events do recognize the loyalty of an employee's service to an organization. In saying that, research has suggested that recognizing service alone will have little impact on moving the needle of employee engagement.

### Mission and Values Awards

The inclusion of awards that are aligned with the mission and values of an organization is another positive recognition vehicle, which not only rewards employees for contributing to your organization's mission and values, it positively reinforces and brands the mission and values internally and externally.

### "Wall of Fame"—Symbolic Visual Recognition

Some organizations have a "wall of fame," where employees of the month/year or winners of awards have their pictures and positive contribution stories publicly displayed or highlighted on websites and social media, recognizing their accomplishments and contributions to their organization.

## The Next Level

Asking your employee engagement council and asking employees through employee engagement surveys or task groups what meaningful corporate recognition looks like to them. Employee responses help senior leaders design corporate initiatives, which provide meaningful impact that moves the needle for employee recognition, retention, and engagement.

### Peer-to-Peer Recognition

In addition to direct manager recognition programs and corporate-wide recognition programs, implementing a peer-to-peer recognition strategy where peers recognize each other for going above and beyond the call of duty is a next-level recognition strategy. Many organizations do not understand the additional value and impact of peer-to-peer recognition. Peer recognition is valuable, because employees who work alongside each other on a daily basis are able to see employees at their best. As with direct manager recognition and corporate-wide recognition strategies, peer-to-peer recognition programs increase employee engagement, lower turnover rates, and help round out direct manager recognition and corporate-wide recognition programs by fostering collegiality, trust, and team spirit amongst employees. It also helps motivate employees to continue to do better on future tasks or projects. Organizations that implement peer-to-peer recognition programs see an additional thirty percent increase in engagement scores over organizations that only implement manager or corporate-wide recognition strategies.

Peer-to-peer recognition strategies can be as simple as a "thank you" recognition at weekly meetings, townhalls, or offline employee recognition thank you cards. They can be as complex as implementing a software recognition survey tool where employees are asked which person they want to recognize during that survey period. It is important to consider what percentage of employees do not have regular access to the internet or email when designing your program.

A memorable example of the impact a peer-to-peer recognition strategy can have on your employees was our journey to becoming a Top 100 Employer. Our organization implemented a peer-to-peer recognition strategy, which was an offline program, and included recognition cards that could be filled out by employees or leaders who had seen their peers going above and beyond what was expected of them. The completed recognition card was submitted to management, and the manager would present the employee with both the recognition card and a recognition pin that was designed with our "people-centered" strategic priority logo. Employees would place this recognition pin on their uniforms, clothes, and lanyards. When we implemented this program, the culture shift that occurred was incredible. For example, as I was standing in the cafeteria line waiting to pay for my lunch, I noticed the employee ringing up our lunches had five or six of these recognition pins on her lanyard. This allowed me, as a senior leader, to ask her about what she had done to be recognized by her peers to get all of her recognition pins. Not only was she getting recognized by her peers, her manager, and her senior leaders, but she was also recognized by anyone asking about her recognition pins. The recognition impact of that was incredible and immeasurable.

## And Beyond . . .

As our employee recognition strategies evolved, we recognized the incredible positive impact these strategies had on our employees. Our employee engagement council began to ask what else could be done to recognize the work and contribution of our employees.

We conducted research, which identified several organizations that recognized employees as valued assets. These organizations had evolved their recognition strategies to not only include the basics and next level initiatives, but they also included some of the additional initiatives listed below to help them create a culture where employees felt valued and recognized for their positive contributions. Some examples of these include:

- Tuition reimbursement
- Community involvement opportunities
- Sabbaticals
- Flex-work schedules
- Recognition designed for specific behaviors and values (i.e., if your organization values innovation, strategically recognizing the value/behavior of innovation helps encourage even more innovation)
- Free skills workshops
- Education opportunities
- Paid project time for frontline staff
- Walking in employees' shoes (an excellent opportunity to provide real-time recognition)

Over the course of five years, our organization implemented tuition reimbursement programs, paid time off for education, paid project time for frontline staff, a wellness program, and implemented flex-work schedules during the summer for non-union employees. When our CEO and board put a stake in the ground to be a Top 100 Employer and identified becoming a people-centered organization as a strategic direction, it opened up a world of possibilities as to how to achieve these objectives. Looking back, it was almost magical how we went from a deficit, less-than-ideal employee and leadership culture to one in which we implemented strategies that only the top employee engaged organizations in North America implemented. It was beyond exciting to be a part of the change.

## Growth and Development of Employees as a Recognition Strategy

Although growth and development of employees is not often thought of as a recognition strategy, in a recent Gallup study, organizations that made a strategic investment in employee development reported eleven percent greater profitability and were twice as likely to retain their employees. Understanding and recognizing an employee's strengths instead of the traditional approach of identifying weaknesses, will not only help managers recognize employees, it will also help them develop their individual strengths and provide them with opportunities to learn and grow. Recognition of an employees' strengths, while providing growth and development opportunities, creates the best conditions for your employees to do their best work. This will keep your talented employees in your organization, motivated and excited to achieve your organizational goals.

## Performance Evaluations and Recognition

There have been many studies looking at the impact timely feedback has on an employee's performance and the association between an employee's level of engagement and satisfaction. In an organization in which I previously worked, employees identified fair and timely feedback of performance as one of the important drivers of engagement. As a result of their feedback, we included fair and timely feedback as one of our strategic goals. In a 2017 Gallup publication, "Re-Engineering Performance Management," it was noted, "Timely feedback is more likely to be helpful and feel constructive, while delayed feedback seems more like evaluation and criticism of past mistakes." In addition, Gallup's database of sixty-plus million employees demonstrated that when leaders provided timely feedback, as opposed to waiting to provide the feedback during an annual performance review, employees are "three times more likely to be engaged at work, six times more likely to agree that they are motivated to do outstanding work, six times more likely to agree that the feedback is meaningful."

## Recognizing the Effort, Persistence, and Resilience

It is important to recognize the successes and accomplishments of your employees, leaders, and teams. Recognizing their effort, persistence, and resilience is just as important. Cultivating and rewarding resilience in your leaders and employees when things do not go as planned, where obstacles emerge and perhaps a less than desired outcome was achieved, is critical. In most strategies that are implemented, obstacles emerge that could not have been predicted. How your employees and leaders work through these obstacles with resiliency and persistence is pivotal to achieving your organization's goals. Rewarding the effort and resilience is as important as achieving the goal itself. You want leaders who learn from their mistakes, who are comfortable with taking risks, and who do not stay stuck in a rut because that is where they are most comfortable.

## A Mindset of Gratitude

In Chapter 4, we spent time working our way through a gratitude exercise to help you shift to a positive mindset for the purposes of the work to be done in that chapter. Incorporating that same gratitude leadership practice into your daily routine will help you develop a gratitude mindset. Furthermore, this will help you begin to see more and more things to be grateful for. As a senior leader, helping your leaders cultivate a gratitude practice will help them shift to a more positive mindset, which will naturally evolve into how they approach their employees. Beginning meetings with sharing what you are grateful for and asking your leaders to do the same sets the stage for a more positive and productive meeting. This also reinforces to your leaders that what they do provides value and makes a difference to your organization, your employees, and the customers you serve!

Unfortunately, due to the significant workload of managers, they tend to look at employee recognition as another task to check off their never-ending to-do list. Shifting that perspective to one of mindful gratitude is key to your leaders' and your approach as you move forward. Starting and ending your day with what you are grateful for in your leadership position is an incredible asset to your leadership toolkit. Moreover, thinking about employees you are grateful for and the specific actions your employees or leaders did that day, will continue to shift your mindset in a positive direction.

Creating a positive mindset that is specifically focused on gratitude will influence how you authentically recognize your employees. Your beliefs and thoughts regarding employee recognition will influence how your employees perceive the degree of authenticity in which you provide recognition. Taking the time to continuously work on creating a positive mindset that understands the value of genuine employee recognition will impact how you authentically provide that recognition.

Everyone desires to be a part of something that they can positively contribute to and be valued for. Recognizing that contribution corporately and at a departmental level is a key factor for employees to feel valued and connected. In return, this will increase their engagement, retention, and achieve your organizational goals.

## ————— Key Takeaways from Chapter 12 —————

- Ask employees what meaningful recognition is to them.
- Understand that money alone is not a recognition strategy.
- Recognize the power of a "thank you" in real time.
- Understand the importance of the role of a direct manager in recognizing employees.
- Recognition strategies can help reinforce your organization's values, improve retention, and positively impact your bottom line.
- Employee perks such as Ping-Pong tables does not equal recognition.
- Use the value of peer-to-peer recognition.
- Recognize persistence, effort, and resilience in addition to successful goal achievement.
- Understand the value of using timely feedback to recognize employees (as opposed to waiting for their performance evaluation).
- Provide employees with growth and development opportunities as a recognition tool.
- Develop a mindset of gratitude.
- Understand the link between how you feel about recognition and how the employees perceive authenticity in your appreciation.

**Chapter 13:**

# Celebrate. Team Building. Celebrate.

*"Remember to celebrate milestones as you*
*prepare for the road ahead."*

**— Nelson Mandela**

Although celebrating and recognizing employees can be thought of as one and the same, I decided to dedicate a chapter specifically to the importance of the celebrating milestones of service or project completion, achievements, and successes.

If you are anything like me, you quickly move on from one project to the next without taking time to pause and acknowledge the work you just accomplished. You certainly are not taking time to celebrate the milestones you achieved or your successes. You also know there is always more to do. There are always more projects to start and finish, more problems to solve, more research on best practices to conduct, more targets to hit, and more goals to create and achieve. You can make a detailed list of all the areas that are still in need of improvement. The thought of taking any time to celebrate (and certainly plan a celebration) when you could be jumping ahead to implement the next strategy may not seem a productive or valuable use of your time.

During an employee engagement council meeting, as we discussed the recent notification that we were shortlisted to be a Top 100 Employer, I had a wake-up call when our employees stated that they wanted to celebrate that achievement. I wanted to wait until we achieved the actual designation. Rightfully so, our employees were insistent that we celebrate this milestone of being shortlisted. As I prepared to respond to the employees regarding why we couldn't or shouldn't celebrate the shortlisting, I looked at their faces and saw them beaming with pride—pride that came from being shortlisted. To them, this shortlisting (let alone what we would eventually achieve, the Top 100 Employer designation) was accomplishment enough. To these employees, many who had worked for the organization decades longer than I had, would never have dreamt that their organization could even be considered a Top 100 Employer. Nor could they have ever imagined they would be an integral part of that journey by participating as a member of the employee engagement council. As I looked around at the closely connected team and considered how it had originally been a disjointed group made up of different classifications of employees and leaders, I stopped in my tracks and acquiesced to their need and desire to accomplish this important milestone . . . and celebrate we did!

This lesson taught me the importance of spending time to celebrate, and not only the end-goal achievement of an employees' service to an organization, but to also celebrate milestones along the way toward achieving a goal or project. Celebrating comes in many forms, from big recognition events of employees' service to celebrating at lunch for a departmental goal achieved.

So how much does celebration help with this employee retention problem that we began the book discussing? As it turns out, a lot. Celebrating achievements, successes, and milestones helps build a sense of community, deepens relationships, strengthens the team, and fosters camaraderie. In turn, celebrating increases employee engagement and reduces turnover. With recognition, there have been many studies to support the fact that celebrations of milestones, long services, successes, and accomplishments are directly linked to employee engagement, retention, and team building.

As a personal example, our annual recognition banquets (held in addition to recognizing the service of our employees) were designed to be an amazing celebration of their contributions to our organization. Managers, leaders, and participants in this event who were not being recognized came and enjoyed the event because it was such an amazing celebration of all our employees. At the request of our CEO, Phil, we introduced our mission awards for individuals and teams to the celebration event and treated the awards like the Oscars. This heightened the celebration of an already-successful event to something even more spectacular. It was always fun to see the reactions of those new board members, physicians, and employees who were invited to the annual banquet as nominees for the mission awards and who had not attended the banquet. They were always blown away by the hooting, cheering, and applauding from the leaders and team members celebrating the employees receiving their milestone pins!

Another moving part of the annual recognition banquet was inviting the celebrated employees' spouses and family members. Being able to thank the family members directly for supporting their spouses was meaningful and impactful to the families. When I had the honor to emcee a number of these events for years at several organizations, I was always moved by the stories of those receiving their long-service pins and the team support they had from their peers. I have lost count of the goosebumps and moments that moved me to tears during these amazing celebrations.

Celebrating milestones, big and small, fosters team building in ways that formal team building retreats and exercises can never achieve. Celebrations organically help form and strengthen relationships through the shared achievement and milestone celebrations. You can get to know your coworkers and leaders in a different light, a light of celebration and fun.

Celebrations should be tailored in a way that best suits your organization. In addition to the basic celebration of birthdays and work anniversaries, I have seen the not-so-basic celebration of milestones. Some organizations celebrate a ninety-day new hire achievement. Employees are celebrated when they achieve their ninetieth day of employment and end their probationary status. They are given something special from the organization to wear to mark their milestone and are welcomed into their official status. In addition, I have seen organizations go to great lengths to celebrate a long-service employee of thirty or even forty or fifty years of employment. Other organizations take advantage of their internal and external communication vehicles, such as newsletters, townhalls, press releases, and social media platforms to celebrate their employees' service, accomplishments, and organization-wide milestones and achievements. As in previous chapters, the key here is to ask your employees what is meaningful to them. What you might think is worthy of celebration might look different for your employees. Ask your employees how they would like to celebrate because all teams and departments have a unique micro-culture and will want to celebrate different achievements unique to them in a way that represents their team culture.

Celebrations can take many shapes, sizes, and forms. In my career, there have been plenty of times when fundraising events, foundation galas, volunteer activities, and community events all served as opportunities for team building and celebrating. Having teams participate in community challenges is a fun way to get to know your employees and leaders in a different way. This builds teams across different parts and silos of your organization in a way that you cannot do otherwise. It allows you to celebrate any wins, along with the sheer fun of participating in the event. Community events such as relay bike races, scavenger hunts, mud runs, home builds, 5K races, and golf tournaments not only give back to your community but also raise money in a fun way.

What about celebrating with money or employee bonuses? As with recognition, there are many studies that show that monetary recognition/celebration does not move the needle on employee engagement. A "thank you" and other recognition strategies, including celebrating milestones achieved and successes, do far more for employee engagement, team building, and retention than monetary rewards alone. Certainly, in addition to thoughtful and meaningful retention and celebration strategies, a monetary recognition bonus program can supplement your other strategies.

## Role of the Manager and the Importance of Departmental Celebrations

As mentioned earlier, all of us want to be part of something bigger, something we can be proud of. There is also the need for us to feel like we are part of a family, a community. It is much harder to voluntarily resign when you belong to a family or a community. Department members within a positive culture are a family, and organizations with a positive culture are a community. Managers are busy and overloaded, getting pulled in multiple directions and like senior leaders, many of them do not understand the value of creating opportunities and dedicating time and energy to celebrating. Coaching your leaders regarding the importance of creating formal and informal opportunities to celebrate at a departmental level is fundamental in creating family and team environments. Celebrations are easy, low-hanging fruit for your managers to incorporate into their leadership practices.

## Mindset of Celebration

Authenticity is critical when recognizing employees and certainly when celebrating them. Ensuring you are in the right mindset when planning and attending these events is essential. Employees can pick up the vibes of leaders who are not being authentic and are "phoning it in." Planning a token celebration event because you feel it is what must be done, as opposed to being in the positive mindset to celebrate your employees' milestones, will do you more harm than not having a celebration event at all. Incorporating moments of mindfulness and an "attitude of gratitude" throughout your day, with the mindset that your employees are who you are in service to, will help align you to your vison of your ideal senior leader self when planning and authentically attending these events.

Similarly to walking in your employees' shoes, celebration events require social interaction with frontline employees. Many leaders tend to avoid these situations because they are introverted, insecure, self-conscious, and/or generally feel awkward, not sure what to say. Some leaders are fearful of being confronted or exposed (imposter syndrome at work again). If you are one of these leaders, in addition to instilling a mindfulness practice into your daily routine where you practice gratitude and envision your ideal senior leader self when you are at your best, as we did in Chapter 4, you can change your perspective into one where you are of service. You can also look for a good coach who can work with you on your confidence, shyness, and imposter syndrome struggles. In addition, there are many online resources available to help you overcome these feelings and help you feel more confident so you can socialize with your employees.

Yes, celebrating and team building while honoring milestones and achievements are important activities to not only recognize the accomplishments of the great work your team has accomplished but also help build your teams and lay the solid foundation for stronger, more trusting relationships motivated for the work and future successes.

——————— **Key Takeaways from Chapter 13** ———————

- It is important to celebrate milestones along the way in addition to successes.
- Take the time to celebrate the achievements and successes when they occur.
- Celebrations positively reinforce expected behaviors and performance.
- Celebrations build community and family.

- Ask employees what meaningful celebration means to them.
- Managers have an important role in creating and participating in departmental celebration.
- Authenticity is paramount when attending celebration events.
- Having a positive mindset of gratitude when participating authentically in celebrations is essential.

**Chapter 14:**

# Take the Leap

## What If This Actually Works?

What motivated you to pick up this book? Was it the constant churn of employees through your organization? Was it the nagging feeling there is a better way to lead? Was it a sense of disconnection with those you lead? Regardless of the reason you picked up this book, you have successfully worked your way through the chapters. How are you feeling? Are you seeing the possibility of a different approach to leadership? One in which you are in service to those you lead, seeing the world through your employees' eyes and experiencing the reality of your employees' working conditions firsthand? Are you feeling inspired to lead with a positive mindset where all is possible? Or are you feeling overwhelmed by the changes you must make to get there? Perhaps you are wondering where to start? Knowing that you should start somewhere, but not quite sure how to pull yourself out of the daily churn of work and firefighting to move into this new space and style of leadership. No matter what you are experiencing, this is where you are in your leadership journey; any one of these feelings is perfectly normal and expected.

If you made it this far into the book, you know what you are reading has truth to it. The concepts and leadership philosophies resonate with you. Perhaps reading this book helped you identify how you can better connect with your employees and serve them in ways you hadn't thought of or hadn't thought of in a long time. Maybe this book spoke to your inner drive and purpose regarding why you became a leader in the first place.

It may be true that many people who read leadership or non-fiction self-help books struggle to implement what they have read. I am here to tell you that it is possible for you to resolve your employee retention and engagement problems, create value as a senior leader, and achieve your organization's goals on your own or with help. The cost to you as a leader to stay where you are is too great. Additionally, the cost to your leadership team, your employees, and your organization is too significant not to take the leap and begin something new. Your blinders are now off; you cannot unknow what you just learned. You can choose to avoid action, or you can choose to act. This is your decision to make. Take any action, even a small one of gratitude for your role as a senior leader, to begin your transformation and create an environment where your employees feel valued and know that their contribution to your organization is significant and meaningful.

Several times during my career, I was where you are today. I felt tired, uninspired, and disconnected from my leaders and team. It was at those times that I would remember why I became a leader in the first place. I reflected on why I wanted to lead. When I remembered my "why," my purpose—to improve the working conditions of those I serve, so they can do their best work and be proud of their contribution and organization—I found my way again. Back to the frontlines, walking in the shoes of those I served. Without fail, as I shadowed my employees by walking in their shoes, I miraculously reconnected to my calling as a leader. I was grateful for the opportunity to see the incredible commitment my employees had to making a difference for our customers. As a result, I became renewed in my commitment to serve them, listen to them, and do whatever I could to make a difference in their working conditions so they felt valued and could do their best work.

Although walking in my employees' shoes throughout my senior leadership career never let me down, there were many times where I got caught up in everything that had to be accomplished and lost my way. I would defer it in response to (what I thought were) more pressing issues. Not walking in the shoes of my employees would catch up with me, and I would find myself uninspired and not being my most leaderful self. Like with exercise, once I showed up and walked in my employees' shoes (did my workout), I was always grateful for doing so. I became renewed and inspired to reconnect with my employees and make a difference for them. You, too, will feel the same.

Failure to take the leap, staying mired in the status quo or worse, the continuation of the vicious cycle of losing your employees, hiring new ones, and onboarding them while your current staff feels overburdened, burned out, and resentful, should be the reason you take the leap to move forward. Why continue with the status quo? That has led to the pain and suffering you, your leaders, and your employees experience at the hands of the churn of lost employees. There is a world of connection, engagement, retention, and organizational success waiting for you on the other side.

Perhaps you intuitively understand that you should engage with your employees and listen to their feedback; yet, you feel intimidated by what you might hear from them, by what you may see, or by the reality of the conditions of the frontlines. Yes, I understand that it feels more comfortable to sit in your office and in meetings, feeling busy while you accomplish your to-do list for that day. I have been there, many times. Facing your fear of potential feedback from your employees and seeing their working conditions through their eyes is the first step to transforming yourself as a leader and transforming the culture, a culture in which your employees' work is valued and your employees are engaged and want to continue to be part of your team. Yes, there will be times when it will be hard to hear the feedback from your leaders and/or your employees. Yes, it will be hard to see the impact of your decision-making when you did not factor in the feedback of your employees. Yes, there will be times when it will be difficult to see your employees' difficult working environment, one you helped create. I have been there; yet, without moving into the space of discomfort, the change you desire, the change your leaders want, and the change your employees desperately crave will not occur. You will continue to face the downward trend of poor performance, dissatisfaction, and ultimately resignations from your team members, or sadly, your employees will resign their effort and stay on your team, barely performing.

The great news is to move forward, you do not need any financial resources and you can start today, this minute even. Simply take the time to be grateful for having completed this book; be grateful for your role as a senior leader, for your leadership team, and for those you serve. In the past, you have maintained the status quo.

Now is your time to make significant, life-changing impact to your team, by creating value as a senior leader to your employees, organization, and customers by taking the next step and making the leap. By taking time to visualize the ideal senior leader you want and know you can be, you can start this journey now.

Put this book down and think of all the reasons you are grateful, and visualize yourself leading in a way of service to your employees—connecting with them, listening to them, and engaging them in advance for feedback about decisions, seeing the world from their perspective, recognizing and valuing their contributions, and celebrating their achievements along the way. Take a moment now to reflect on these things.

Do you now feel that perhaps you can take the leap? Yes, you can! I am more than confident that once you take that leap and jump in with both feet first, your retention issues will be behind you. In front of you will be the ideal senior leader you know you can be, creating value by leading an engaged and connected high-performing team, one loyal to you and your organization. By creating a culture that values the perspectives and voices of your employees, your team will go above and beyond for their customers, committed to meeting their needs while contributing to the successful achievement of your organizational goals.

## Chapter 15:

# This Is Not the End.
# This Is the Beginning.

As with all journeys, this, too, must come to an end. However, this is only the beginning of your transformation as a senior leader who creates value by connecting with your engaged employees, keeping them on your high-performing team, excited to contribute to achieving your organizational goals, and driving your organization's strategy forward. In my experience, employee engagement is a journey, one that is never-ending and always changing. As expectations of employees, customers, new stakeholders on the board, and the marketplace are always changing, your organization is fluid and employee engagement is as well. You are now equipped with the tools, tactics, and strategies needed to ride the waves of organizational and employee engagement change.

You are taking the steps to prioritize the optimization of your employees' experience, which will help you increase productivity and customer satisfaction. Through authentic connection, engagement, and retention of your people, your organization will create a competitive advantage, the key to the success of your business.

We have covered a lot of ground these past fourteen chapters, beginning with the challenge of retaining your employees. You discovered that even though you had high turnover, there was a lurking problem. You had employees who checked out and became disengaged; yet, they stayed with your team. As you learned ways to carve time out of your schedule for the purposes of understanding "why" solving your employee retention problem was important to you and what leaving it unresolved would cost, you learned mind-setting techniques to help you be grateful for the leadership position you are currently in. Despite the retention and engagement challenges you currently have begun to face. You now understand that being in a position of service to those you lead is one of the greatest privileges you have as a senior leader.

Taking the time to envision who you are as the ideal senior leader you know you can be, you start to feel moments of inspiration, understanding the possibility of all that can be realized when you begin to remove your limiting beliefs. Moments of joy begin to spark as you shake off what feels like the leadership burden of the past, knowing you can lead as you have always wanted to or as you did long ago.

As you pour through the data, metrics, surveys, and comments available to you, a picture comes into focus as to why your employees are leaving; or worse yet, learning that your employees are staying and doing the bare minimum of what is required of them. Getting clear about your employees' reasons for leaving or "why" they are disengaged might be difficult as you begin to see the reality of how they perceive their working conditions. Learning mindset tools and techniques to review this information, without judgment because the past is the past, has helped you to see the gorilla hiding in plain sight and provided you with clarity about how to build a strategy to address your employees' needs. Being open to understanding your employees' perspective is the key to unlocking your employees' highest potential and engaging them in their work.

With a deeper appreciation that employee engagement is not just a human resources buzzword or responsibility, you understand how it impacts key business drivers, such as customer satisfaction, revenue, shareholder value, and profitability. You now see the additional value (aside from employee retention) of making employee connection and engagement a priority.

Finding time and energy to focus on fixing your retention issues may have felt impossible before you began reading this book. Now armed with the perspective that this is the *work* to do, you know that you will repurpose your time to create an environment where your employees feel valued, connected, and engaged so they are less likely to leave your team or organization. With your new priority and focus dedicated to doing the *work,* you are able to align your calendar, activities, and meetings to the priority of engaging with your employees, listening to them, and seeing the world through their eyes.

You have learned the single most important thing to do to connect with your employees, by walking in their shoes or shadowing them. Realizing how meaningful and transformative this practice would be for you as well as your employees. Letting go of the fear, getting outside of your comfort zone, and facing the reality of what the frontlines may hold for you, you now are in position to create significant value as a senior leader. You are ready to see that reality and recognize the outstanding work your employees do on a daily basis in spite of the conditions they work in. You are aware of the importance of authentically listening to employee feedback. You truly value their opinions as to what improvements can be made to help them do the best possible work for your customers.

Knowing that there is always more on a leader's plate than there is time to do it, you learned new, perhaps forgotten, tools and tactics for purposeful action that will move the needle on both employee engagement and your organizational goals. Recognizing that effective communication with employees is the cornerstone of employee engagement, you have become aware of the many communication vehicles available to ensure employees understand how they contribute and positively impact your organizational goals. As a senior leader you acknowledge the importance of your role in creating a culture of transparency and trust, conscious of how leaders and employees look to you as a role model of aligning your words with action.

Realizing how powerful the fundamental leadership strategy of engaging employees and asking for their feedback is in advance of making decisions, you understand how this simple philosophy can make a significant difference regarding how your employees feel valued and heard. Additionally, you appreciate how employees can support, with minimal resistance, decisions they had input into. In fact, you can now envision scenarios where your employees, instead of your leadership team, successfully draft policies or guidelines.

By simply asking your employees for their opinion and feedback on subjects that pertain to them, you can see how effective this strategy is to building trusting and lasting relationships within your team. Learning how you can design meaningful recognition strategies based on employee feedback that aligns with your organization's mission and strategic, operational, and departmental plans, you now understand that these positive reinforcement strategies are a win-win for your employees, yourself, and your organization.

You now see the value of taking the time to celebrate milestones achieved along the way. Laying the foundation for further work ahead. You see how celebrations come with the benefits of building stronger, high-performing teams across silos, helping your employees feel proud to be a part of something bigger than just their contributions alone. Increasing connection, engagement, and retention resultantly follows. Summarily, you can appreciate the exponential momentum and traction that occurs when employees steer the engagement strategy across an organization.

Lastly, you see the value of continuously paying attention with intention to your thoughts, actions, conversations and the work you do. You are now aware of how creating a positive mindset can help you achieve all that is possible and all that you desire to accomplish for yourself as a senior leader, your employees, and your organization. Furthermore, you now know how to identify limiting beliefs and have developed skills to prevent these thoughts from deterring your goals.

As we close this chapter of this book, my wish for you is that you connect or reconnect with those you lead and serve by walking in your employees' shoes. Seeing their experiences through their eyes, you can improve their working conditions, while supporting them in their desire to do their best work. With this understanding of the reality of the front lines, you are now equipped with the information you need to create value as a senior leader by connecting, engaging, and retaining your high-performing employees as you work with purpose and passion toward achieving your organization's goals.

I am certain you will find more value, joy, and satisfaction in your leadership role, while transforming your employees' lives and work experience by making a difference in how they feel about your organization.

As you begin this new chapter in your leadership journey, feel free to reach out, ask questions, and inquire about how I can be of service to you. I'm wishing you all the best as you embark on this important, life-changing, and transformational work!

# Acknowledgments

hope by reading this book you walk away with the inspiration to connect with your employees more deeply, by seeing the reality of your organization through their eyes. As outlined by research and by the information in the chapters, the benefits of connecting with your employees are exponential. None are as great, however, as the honor and privilege you will feel by mindfully walking in your employees' shoes.

I want to first thank all the employees who allowed me to walk in their shoes and/or shadow them. I walked away from each one of those experiences in awe of the dedication those employees gave to their patients, their customers, and to our organizations. I am grateful for their openness with me, teaching me at times many valuable lessons that I have carried with me throughout my career.

There are many leaders, friends and family I would like to acknowledge; without them, I would not be the person and leader I am today. Dr. K. Adeli, who accepted me as a fourth-year biochemistry student for my honors thesis. Spending that year working for Dr. Adeli taught me the importance of applied learning. He was a patient professor who had seen intelligence in me that I perhaps had not seen in myself. With his guidance, my research was able to contribute new knowledge to the study of apolipoproteins, giving me confidence in my abilities to apply theory to practice. I would not have begun my journey into healthcare leadership without his decision to take a chance on me and bring me onto his research team. Jennifer Y., my first mentor. Without the generosity of her time, late evenings in her office and her curiosity as to the reality of the frontlines, I would not have understood the important value of connecting with employees.

Bernie Blais, for his determined passion to bring leadership development into every organization he worked for. Thank you for taking a chance on me and for bringing me on your senior team! Ken Tremblay for his brilliant organizational design that afforded me the opportunity to lead at a senior level a clinical, corporate, and human resources portfolio. His mentorship, incredible knowledge, and vision to achieve being a best-in-class organization made me the senior leader I am today. Karen, my right and left hand during the most important parts of my senior leadership career. Your dedication, expertise, writing skills, and organizational capabilities helped our organizations achieve their goals. During our time together, I never felt that I could adequately articulate your contribution to me personally, professionally, and to our organizations. Linda Moore and Brad Quinn, the founders of tng, you were instrumental in my evolution as a leader. Your impact on me and all those who had the blessing to participate in the Leadership Discovery Experience is immeasurable and longstanding. Dr. Debashis Chatterjee, your wisdom and love for leaders, leadership, and humanity not only inspired the creation of the Leadership Discovery Experience, but it inspired me personally. Taking the time to reflect on leadership while writing this book, I had even more appreciation of how your teachings and contributions shaped my leadership journey. Beth H., throughout writing this book, you were always on my mind. Your people-centered leadership style inspired me from afar to create a leadership message that you and other people-centered leaders like you, would value. Your never-ending commitment to your employees and leaders is the best example of servant leadership I have come across. Through your advocacy and celebration of your people, you have not only touched your employees' lives, you have transformed them! Sarah P., your big thinking, innovative and fearless approach to leadership always stretched my somewhat process-oriented management style. You are one of the most talented and intellectual leaders in healthcare and I continue to be in awe of the breadth and depth of your knowledge.

My fellow LDE participants. You know who you are. I am forever grateful to be a part of your leadership community. Our leadership journey together was nothing short of magical. I am still in awe today as to how much I have learned from all of you. Each one of you is whole, creative, and resourceful. I am hoping today that you are standing in the fire and creating the conditions for other leaders to emerge. Thank you for accepting the challenge with me to dive deeper into ourselves to serve others. I am forever transformed as a result of having known all of you.

My editing team Cory and Bethany, thank you for your continuous flexibility, creativity, and support to help me reach the finish line, especially when life was throwing many obstacles to prevent me from getting there. My print publication editor, Cortney Donelson, I appreciate your fine touches on my manuscript! Morgan James Publishing, thank you for your support of my book and my vision to for senior leaders to authentically connect with their employees.

Finally, to my family who has supported me in this new chapter in my career. Without having the opportunity to step back from senior leadership, to support our family at home, I would not have ever thought writing a book, let alone having it published would be possible. Your flexibility in shifting our routines to accommodate my writing and editing of my book helped me realize that I could stay at home to support our family and also provide value professionally. Tyson, in the last weeks of editing, your analytical skills were nothing short of miraculous. Your ability to help synthesize and make sense out of my lengthy sentences provided clarity and insight to my key messages that would otherwise be lost in the words on paper. Thank you for your help and support during the many late nights, getting it done.

My parents, thank you for your love and for providing me with a life that allowed me to pursue my passions, even when those pursuits meant I would be further away from home. My sisters, Hollie and Dawn, who taught me the value of delegation at a young age. Thank you for tolerating the antics of your older sister! To my niece and nephew, thank you for letting me be your self-proclaimed "favorite aunt!" Josh, your insight, humor and perspectives on music, golf, travel and life have broaden my own perspectives. Austyn, you are an amazing hero and role model for Savannah. You are such a smart, strong (and flexible!) young woman. I look forward to watching you continue to grow. You both have brought such joy and love to our family.

And finally, my beautiful, courageous, leaderful, loving daughter, Savannah Grace. You are the most precious gift I have ever been blessed with. You have taught me so much about joy, patience, selflessness and have helped me find what is truly important in life. Unconditional Love.

# Thank You!

Thank you for reading my book, *Creating Value as a Senior Leader*. I know that you are on the path to optimizing your full potential as a senior leader to create and provide value to your employees and organization. Through connecting with your employees, I am confident you will make a difference in the lives of those you serve, all while achieving your organization's goals.

As has been the case throughout my career as a CEO and executive, I am sincerely passionate about helping leaders establish a competitive advantage by creating the conditions for their employees to do their best work. I would love to hear your feedback at shona@shonaelliott.org about how you create value as a senior leader.

Realizing your full potential to create value as a senior leader with the many competing priorities you have is a delicate balance and I want to support you in any way possible. If I can be of any service to you, I invite you to a sixty-minute, complimentary conversation with me. Please schedule time for our conversation by going to my website www.shonaelliott.org or by emailing me at shona@shonaelliott.org. I wish you all the best in this next chapter of your leadership journey.

With gratitude,
Shona

## About the Author

Shona Elliott is an experienced senior leader who is passionate about helping other senior leaders authentically connect and engage with their greatest assets—their employees—for the purposes of increasing employee retention, employee engagement, and achieving an organization's strategic goals. As a former CEO, of a  healthcare technology and supply chain organization, with fifteen years of senior leadership experience in healthcare, Shona understands the many challenges and competing priorities of busy executives. Having been in their shoes, designing and successfully implementing her organizations' strategic plans, she recognized and harnessed the power of employee engagement to achieve her organizations' goals.

Throughout her fifteen years as a senior leader—both in healthcare and for-profit organizations in Canada and the United

States—Shona has a proven track record helping organizations achieve cultural renewal and operational excellence with a people-centered focus. Through connection with leaders and employees, Shona has led an organization through the process to achieve two Top 100 Employer designations. Shona has extensive expertise in strategic planning, pandemic planning & response, crisis leadership, human resources, operations, transformational leadership, organizational development, clinical operations, technology & supply chain and quality management.

Shona previously worked and lived in Southwestern Ontario, Canada, where she obtained her Bachelor of Science, honors degree in biochemistry. Shona also holds an MBA from NYIT, an advanced program certificate in human resources management from the University of Toronto and obtained her certification as an ISO 9000 auditor. She now lives with her family in Edmond, Oklahoma. Shona is an avid golfer, having golfed six out of the seven continents. In addition, she is a novice biohacker, a cautious skier, a world traveler, as well as a food and cooking enthusiast.

# Endnotes

## Chapter 4

Tae-Youn Park and Jason D. Shaw, "Turnover Rates and Organizational Performance: A Meta-Analysis," *Journal of Applied Psychology* 98, no. 2 (2013): 268–309.

Robert A. Emmons, *Gratitude Works! A Twenty-One-Day Program for Creating Emotional Prosperity.* San Francisco: Jossey-Bass, 2013, 10.

## Chapter 5

Richard S. Wellins, Paul Bernthal, and Mark Phelps, "Employee Engagement: The Key to Realizing Competitive Advantage," *Development Dimensions International, Inc.,* https://www.ddiworld.com/resources/library/white-papers-monographs/employee-engagement.

"The State of Employee Engagement in 2019," HR.com, 2019, https://www.hr.com/en/resources/free_research_white_papers/

Jim Harter and Annemarie Mann, "The Right Culture: Not Just About Employee Satisfaction," *Gallop*: *Workplace,* 12 April 2017, https://www.gallup.com/workplace/236366/right-culture-not-employee-satisfaction.aspx.

"If You're Not Looking for It, You Probably Won't See It," Press Release, Brigham and Women's Hospital, 19 July 2013, https://www.brighamandwomens.org/about-bwh/newsroom/press-releases-detail?id=1520.

Randall J. Beck and Jim Harter, "Why Great Managers Are So Rare," *Gallop:* Workplace, https://www.gallup.com/workplace/231593/why-great-managers-rare.aspx.

## Chapter 6

Tracy, Brian, "How To Delegate The Right Tasks To The Right People: Effective Management Skills For Leadership Success," Brian Tracy International, 2019, https://www.briantracy.com/blog/leadership-success/how-to-delegate-the-right-tasks-to-the-right-people-effective-management-skills-for-leadership-success/6/.

## Chapter 7

Darrell Rigby and Barbara Bilodeau, "Management Tools and Trends," Bain and Co., 10 June 2015, https://www.bain.com/insights/management-tools-and-trends-2015/.

## Chapter 9

Natalie Hackbarth and David Weisser, "How to Conduct Employee Focus Groups," Quantum Workplace, http://resources.quantumworkplace.com/TeamPulseIdeas/Resources-Whitepapers-How-to-Conduct-Employee-Focus-Groups.pdf.

## Chapter 10

"Capitalizing on Effective Communication," Watson Wyatt Worldwide, 2009/2010, http://benefitcommunications. com/upload/downloads/Capitalizing_on_Effective_ Communication_-_Towers_Watson_survey.pdf.

"The Impact of Employee Engagement on Performance," *Harvard Business Review*, 2003, 3.

Nicole, "The Most Important Thing in Communication is Hearing What Isn't Said—Peter F. Drucker," *Rants and Revelations* Blog, 26 September 2010, https://rantsandrevelations.wordpress. com/2010/09/.

## Chapter 12

Annamarie Mann and Nate Dvorak, "Employee Recognition: Low Cost, High Impact," *Gallop:Workplace*, 28 June 2016, https:// www.gallup.com/workplace/236441/employee-recognition-low-cost-high-impact.aspx.

Martin Dewhurst, Matthew Guthridge, and Elizabeth Mohr, "Motivating People: Getting Beyond Money,"McKinsey and Company, 2019, https://www.mckinsey.com/business-functions/organization/our-insights/motivating-people-getting-beyond-money.

Josh Bersin, "New Research Unlocks the Secret of Employee Recognition," *Forbes*, 13 June 2012, https://www.forbes. com/sites/joshbersin/2012/06/13/new-research-unlocks-the-secret-of-employee-recognition/#36761ca15276.

Greg Bartlomiejczuk, "How do Recognition Programs Impact Employee Engagement and how have Companies with a Large Companies with a Large Global Footprint Structured Such Programs to Drive Results?" Cornell University, 2015,

https://digitalcommons.ilr.cornell.edu/cgi/viewcontent.
cgi?article=1074&context=student.

Susan Sorenson, "How Employee Engagement Drives Growth,"
Gallup: Workplace, 20 June 2013, https://www.gallup.com/
workplace/236927/employee-engagement-drives-growth.
aspx.

Ben Wigert and Jim Harter, "Re-Engineering Performance
Management," *Gallup, Inc.,* 2017.

CPSIA information can be obtained
at www.ICGtesting.com
Printed in the USA
JSHW031005110321
12420JS00011B/36